About Us

About Us

The 1973 Childcraft Annual

An Annual Supplement to
Childcraft—The How and Why Library

Field Enterprises Educational Corporation

Chicago London Paris Rome Stuttgart Sydney Tokyo Toronto

Acknowledgments

The publishers of *Childcraft—The How and Why Library*
gratefully acknowledge the courtesy of the following
publishers, persons, and organizations for permission to
use copyrighted illustrations appearing in this volume. Full
illustration acknowledgments appear on pages 296–297.

Page 233: Illustration by N.C. Wyeth from *The Boy's King
Arthur* edited by Sidney Lanier; © 1917, renewed
1945, Charles Scribner's Sons (from the collection
of Jack Webb)

Page 287: Eliot Elisofon, *Life* © Time Inc.

Page 288: Bill Ray, *Life* © Time Inc.

Preface

Dear Reader,

Please accept this invitation to visit us. Plan to join our families for a day, a week, or for as long as you like. You won't have any trouble finding us. We live in Afghanistan and Zaire and all the countries in between.

We want you to meet all of us—our mothers and fathers, sisters and brothers, grandmothers and grandfathers. Live in our houses, eat our food, wear our clothes. Let us tell you what we believe and how we worship.

Help us in our work. Play our games and go on vacations with us. Sit with us in our classrooms. Learn our languages. Sing our songs, dance our dances, listen to our stories and riddles.

Learn our customs. Live by our rules and laws. Be with us when we are welcomed into the world. Watch the many ways we celebrate the end of childhood. Be a guest at our weddings. Weep with us in our moments of sorrow. Laugh with us in our moments of joy.

Please come soon. We want to meet you, to know all about you. And we want you to know *About Us*.

About Us

Contents

Who Are We?

We're all the people in the world.

We live everywhere—in crowded cities and tiny towns. We live on white, frozen plains and in hot, green forests. We live in deserts, on mountainsides, and on islands in the seas.

We come in many colors. Some of us have warm, tan skins like sunlight on sand. Some of us have deep brown skins, like rich chocolate. Some of us have rosy pink skins, the color of the sky at dawn. And some of us have skins that are touched with the red glint of copper or the tawny gleam of gold. We come in many colors, and all the colors are beautiful.

Our eyes and hair are different colors, too. We have blue eyes or brown eyes or gray eyes or green eyes. Our hair may be blonde or brown or red or black. It may be straight or it may be curly.

We come in many different sizes and shapes. Some of us are tall and some of us are short. Some of us are thin and some of us are stout.

We have many different ways of life. We have many different beliefs and customs. We like different kinds of foods. We build our houses in different ways. But we're very much alike in many important ways. We must all have food. We all want to be comfortable and happy. We all need love and friendship. We all like beautiful things.

We belong to many different families, groups, tribes, and nations. But we all belong to one big family— the human family of nearly four billion people—for we all have the same ancestors.

We're *us*—the people of the planet Earth.

a house in the United States

We need shelter to protect us from the weather.

We need to eat in order to stay alive.

eating a meal in Tunisia

Navaho Indian children

We wear some kind of clothing.

To stay alive

Food, clothing, and shelter are three of our most
important needs. But all of us do not eat the same
kinds of food. We do not wear the same kinds of
clothes. Nor do we live in the same kinds of houses.
You'll find out more about these things in this book.

To get the things we need

We all work to get the things we need. Some of us grow our own food and make our own clothes. Some of us work for money to buy these things. In this book, you will discover some of the ways we earn a living.

We work to get all the things we need.

gathering seaweed in Japan

Alaskan Eskimo children

We all find ways to have fun and enjoy life.

To enjoy life

We all take time out to have fun. We know that
all work and no play makes a dull life. This book tells
about the games we play and some of the many other
ways we find to enjoy ourselves.

To live together

We all live in families. But not all families live in the same way. And everywhere there are rules to make it easier to live and work and play together. In this book you will read about different families. And you will find out about the kinds of rules we live by.

a Lapp family

We live in groups called families.

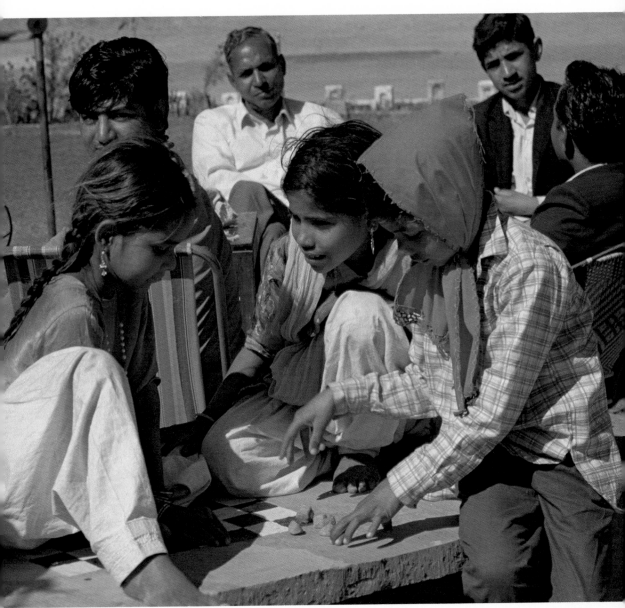

playing a game in India

We have to live and play by rules.

a classroom in Peru

We learn from our families, friends, and teachers.

a telephone booth in Russia

We communicate with one another in many different ways.

To know about our world

We all have to learn about the world we live in. And we have to learn the skills we need for our way of life. We learn from our family, friends, and teachers. We get and give information by listening and talking. We write. We read. We communicate.

As you read this book, you will find out how we learn the many things we need to know. You will find out how we communicate with other people.

a Sicilian donkey cart

We find ways to decorate the things we use.

To make life worth living

We try to make ourselves and the world around us beautiful. We pray for the help we need to love and be kind to one another. In this book you will learn about some of the many ways we do these things.

We find ways to express our deepest beliefs.

a guitar Mass

Botswana

Kwi lives in a hot desert,
so he doesn't wear clothes.
He has no house—his
family travels from place
to place to find food.

What we learn makes the difference

Kwi is six years old. He lives in the Kalahari
Desert in Botswana, Africa. He belongs to a group of
people called Bushmen.

Danny is six, too. He lives on the coast of Maine,
in the Northeastern United States.

It is always hot in Kwi's desert, so he never wears
anything but a string of beads around his neck. Even
his parents and other grown-ups wear few clothes.

Where Danny lives it is often cold. He and his
parents have to wear enough clothes to keep warm.

Kwi has no house. His family moves from place to
place, looking for food. Kwi eats wild animals that his
father hunts, and roots and melons that his mother
finds. He has never tasted, nor even seen, a fish.

Danny's family has lived in the same house for many
years. Living near the ocean, they eat fish often.
Most of their food is bought from stores.

Since he was a baby, Kwi has been taught the ways
of Bushmen by his parents and other people of his
group. He has learned all the beliefs, stories, songs,

United States

Danny lives in a house with his family. He goes to school. His father works for money to buy food and other things the family needs.

and dances that are important to Bushmen. He will never go to school nor learn how to read or write.

Danny learns many things from his parents, too. But he also learns things at church and school. His religion, his games—even his ways of thinking about things—are not the same as Kwi's.

Kwi and Danny look very different. But it isn't the color of their skin or hair, or the things they wear, that makes them different. It's their way of life— their culture—that really makes them different. And culture is a *learned* way of life.

If Danny had been brought up by Kwi's family, he would have learned to live the way Bushmen live. He would like the foods they like. He would do the things they do. He would believe what they believe.

If Kwi had been brought up by Danny's family, he would have learned to live the way Danny's family lives. He would like their foods. He would do the things they do. He would believe what they believe.

People aren't different. It's ways of life that are different. We learn our way of life—our culture— from the people with whom we live and grow up.

**Earth, as photographed
from the Apollo 17 spacecraft.**

Where Did We Come From?

How did the world begin? Where did we come from? People have been puzzling over questions like these for thousands of years.

The answers given in the Bible are perhaps the oldest and best known. But people from every land and every culture have their own story of how the world, and all the things in it, came to be. These stories are filled with things the people thought were important, wonderful, and beautiful. Some of the stories also tell us a great deal about the people who first told them and the places where these people lived.

The newest story is one that scientists from many different cultural backgrounds are still putting together. Most scientists think it is the true story. Some people say it is not. But it, too, is an attempt to explain the things that people everywhere have always wondered about.

An illustration from the Jicarilla Apache story of the creation of the world.

God created Heaven, Earth, and the Seas.

The seven days

"What is the *very* oldest story you know?" Jane asked her grandmother.

Her grandmother thought for a moment. "I guess it must be the story of the Creation, from the Bible."

"How old is it?" Jane wanted to know.

"Why, many people think it was written down about four thousand years ago by a man named Moses," said her grandmother. "Moses was a great Jewish leader who freed the Jewish people from slavery in Egypt. The Biblical story of the Creation is called Genesis, which is a word that means beginning."

Jane sat down on the floor beside her grandmother's chair and crossed her legs. "Tell me the story."

"Before the beginning of things," said her grandmother, "there was no earth and no sky. There was only a great dark emptiness and a great dark ocean of water. God gazed upon the water and thought.

"Then God said, 'Let there be light!' And there was light. It pushed back the darkness and shone upon the water. God called the light Day and the darkness Night. That first time of light and darkness was the first day of the world.

"On the second day, God said, 'Let there be a great sky. Let it divide the waters so that some of the water is above it and some below it.' God called the sky Heaven.

"On the third day, God said, 'Let all the water beneath the sky come together in one place. Let the dry land appear.' The water rushed together and the land appeared, with mountains and valleys. God called the dry land Earth. And the waters He called Seas.

God created plants, the sun, and the moon.

" 'Let the earth grow grass, and plants, and trees, with seeds and fruit,' said God. The earth turned green with growing things.

"On the fourth day, God made the stars, the sun, and the moon. He set them in the sky to separate the day from the night, and to be signs for the seasons and the years.

"On the fifth day, He made all the creatures that live in the water and all the birds that fly in the sky. Then, on the sixth day, He made all the animals that live on the land. Finally, God made a man and a woman in His likeness. 'Have many children and fill the earth with people,' He told them. 'I have made you to be the rulers of the earth.'

"Now the world was finished. God's work was all done and He was pleased with it. So, on the seventh day, He rested."

Grandmother looked down at Jane. "And that's the oldest story I know—the story of the Creation as it's told in the Bible."

God created birds, fish, beasts, and man and woman.

Frost and fire; giants and gods

A white cover of snow hid the ground. It lay on the roofs of the houses and sat in great gobs on the dark-green branches of the fir trees. Sven's nose and cheeks tingled in the icy air. He blew a puff of breath between his lips and watched it turn to steam.

His grandfather smiled at him. "Are you trying to make another Ymir?" he asked.

"Who's Ymir?" Sven wanted to know.

"Well, Ymir was a giant, and the first living thing in the world," said grandfather. "He's in a story our ancestors used to tell—a story of how the world began. We don't believe it any more, of course, but this story, and others like it, is still part of our lives. Many of our customs come from these old Norse stories of gods and heroes and giants. Why, the days Tuesday, Wednesday, and Thursday are named after Norse gods, and Friday is named after a Norse goddess."

"Tell me about Ymir," Sven begged. He loved his grandfather's stories. They were one reason he liked to visit his grandparents in the northern part of Sweden.

"Long ago," the old man began, "where the world is now, there was only a great yawning opening called Ginnungagap.

"South of Ginnungagap was a world of fire. It glowed with light. Heat shimmered over it. Sparks of fire rose up from it and drifted through the air.

"North of Ginnungagap was a world of mist. In its center was a well. Twelve rivers flowed out of the well and ran toward Ginnungagap. The farther they ran, the colder they grew, until finally they turned to ice. The ice fell into Ginnungagap with a noise

like the roar of endless thunder. Slowly, Ginnungagap
filled up with ice and frost and cold, cold mist.

"Then, from the world of fire came floating sparks
and hot winds. The breath of heat met the cold mists
and made steam—just as your warm breath makes
steam on a cold day such as this. Out of the warm
steam was formed a giant, whose name was Ymir, and
a cow, called Audhumla. They were the first
living things."

"What did they live on?" interrupted Sven. "There
was nothing but ice and snow."

"Ymir lived on the milk that Audhumla gave, and Audhumla lived on the salt she licked out of the ice," grandfather explained with a smile.

"Was Ymir one of the Norse gods?" asked Sven.

"No." Grandfather shook his head. "Ymir was the first Frost Giant. He was evil, for the Frost Giants wanted the world for themselves and hated men. But let me finish.

"Ymir lay down to sleep. Out of his body came a man and a woman. They had many children, and these children were the Frost Giants.

"Then, one day as Audhumla was licking the ice, a man's body came out of it! His name was Buri and he created a son, named Bor. Bor married a Frost Giant woman and they had three sons, named Vili, Ve, and Odin. And these three were the first gods.

"Odin and his brothers saw at once that Ymir was evil, so they fought him and killed him. Then, from his body they made this world we live on.

"The land was made from his flesh. The mountains were made from his bones. The sea was made from his blood. From his skull they made the sky. They filled it with sparks from the fire world, to make the sun, moon, and stars.

"As soon as the sun began to shine, grass and trees burst up out of the earth. Then Odin and his brothers made the first man, Ask, out of an ash tree, and the first woman, Embla, out of an elder tree. And Ask and Embla were the father and mother of all the people in the world.

"So that's how our Norse ancestors believed the world began," said grandfather. "Now, let's get back in the house and ask grandma to give us some coffee and cookies!"

A green sprout and a rainbow

It was springtime, and Sayuri was glad. The cherry
trees were in bloom and the warm air was filled
with their fragrance. It really is wonderful, thought
Sayuri, how everything seems to come to life in
the spring. I wonder how it happens? Has it always
been this way, or was it different once?

"Has the world always been here?" she asked her
mother.

Her mother smiled and shook her head. "No, not
always. At one time, long ago, there was no earth,
there was no heaven. All things were mixed together in
a great cloud. Slowly, the clear, light parts of the
cloud rose up and became heaven. The heavy parts of
the cloud sank down and became a lump of muddy
water. That was the beginning of the world."

"Where did all the people come from?" asked Sayuri.

"Between earth and heaven, a pale green sprout, like
a young bamboo plant, began to grow," said her
mother. "It grew swiftly and was very, very strong.
When its flower burst open, it was the First God, the
One Who Made All Things That Last Forever.

"The First God stretched out his hands and created
the first man, Izanagi, and the first woman,
Izanami. He gave them a jeweled spear and said,
'Go now, and finish making the world.'

"The man and woman stepped upon the rainbow, the
floating bridge of heaven that hung above the earth.
Izanagi reached out and dipped the spear into the
muddy water. Then he raised it high. A bit of mud
that had stuck to the spear dropped off. As swiftly as a
shooting star it fell back toward the water. When
it struck the water, it became an island.

"Izanagi and Izanami went down to the island and built a house. There they lived, and together they made the islands of Japan. They also made all the gods and goddesses and, later, the first people who lived upon the islands."

"But where did all the animals come from?" Sayuri asked.

Her mother smiled. "That's another story."

Clouds, winds, and the songs of birds

Storytelling time!

Everyone in the class was excited, because today it was the new boy's turn to tell a story. The new boy was an Indian—a real Apache Indian! Surely he would have a wonderful story to tell!

Even the teacher was curious. "What kind of story do you have for us, Billy?" she asked, when he came up to the front of the room.

He grinned shyly. "A very old story that I heard from a very old man named Pesh-Coo. It is the Jicarilla Apache story of how the world began."

The teacher and the other children settled back to listen, and he began.

"Once, there was no world. There was nothing but darkness, water, and the moving wind. Nothing was alive but the Spirits. They had always been alive.

"The Spirits had great power. They could do anything. They made the earth, who is the mother of all people, animals, and plants. And they made the sky, who is their father.

"The greatest of the Spirits was Black Spirit. He mixed a raindrop with earth and made a bit of mud. From the mud he made all the birds and animals that live upon the earth.

(continued on page 32)

"The birds and animals gathered around him. 'Will you always be with us?' they asked.

" 'No,' answered Black Spirit. 'Some day I must go away and you will never see me again.'

" 'Then make someone like you, who will always be with us,' they pleaded.

"So Black Spirit told them to go to all the places where the wind blew and bring back all the things they could find. They brought pollen, red earth, white stones, blue turquoise, and many other things. Black Spirit took these things and made them into a man. The pollen was the man's flesh, the red earth was his blood, the turquoise became his veins, the white stones were his bones. His hair was made from a black cloud, but when a man grows old, his hair becomes a white cloud.

"When the man was complete, Black Spirit sent a whirlwind into him. The wind whirled through the man's body and brought him to life. Because of that whirlwind, we have little whirls on our fingertips.

" 'He will be lonely,' said the animals. 'You should make a companion for him.'

"So Black Spirit put the man to sleep, to dream of the kind of companion he wanted. The man dreamed that a woman was sitting beside him. When he awoke, his dream had come true.

" 'Let us walk,' said the man to the woman, and they walked together.

" 'Let us run,' said the man, and they ran together.

"Then the man and woman laughed together, because they were happy. The birds were happy, too, so they burst into song. And in memory of that time, the birds still burst into song each day at dawn."

The sky shell and the octopus

"Papa," said Claudine, "what's this?" She was holding the little wooden statue that had stood on a shelf in their living room for as long as she could remember.

"That came from the island of Tahiti, in the South Pacific Ocean," her father told her. "I used to work there, before you were born. It's a statue of the ancient Tahitian god Ta'aroa. According to an old story, he made the world out of a shell."

"How did he do that?" asked Claudine, her eyes round with wonder.

"Let me see if I remember the story." Her father

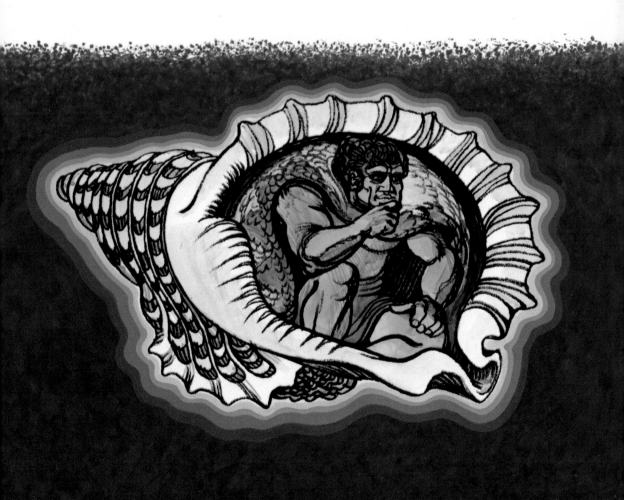

rubbed his chin thoughtfully. "It was told to me by an old, old man. As I remember, it went like this:

"Once, there was no sky, no land, no sea, no sun, no moon, and no stars. There was only emptiness. In the middle of the emptiness was a shell. Inside the shell was Ta'aroa.

"For many ages Ta'aroa sat in his shell and thought. Once he left his shell and looked about, but there was nothing to see. 'This is not good,' said Ta'aroa.

"He made a new shell and sat in it for a few more ages. Then he felt a stirring within himself. He was filled with a wish to make things. So he took the new shell he had made and turned it into the world. He made the old shell into the sky and set it upon the world. He shook his feather cape so that feathers fell onto the earth. They became grass, trees, clumps of bananas, and other growing things.

"Then Ta'aroa made the other gods. The gods looked around, but they couldn't see anything. This was because Tumu-ra-i-feuna, the great spotted octopus, was holding the sky tightly against the earth with his eight arms. The world was like the inside of a closed clamshell.

"So the god Rua killed the octopus with magic. But even though he was dead, Tumu-ra-i-feuna did not let go of the sky. The gods tried to pry his arms loose and push the sky up, but it was no use.

"Finally, they went to Tane, who was the greatest of all gods except for Ta'aroa. With his great ax, Tane cut down huge trees and pushed them between the earth and the sky. Then he tugged and heaved on the trees. At last the sky broke free and light came into the world.

"Then Tane decorated the sky with stars and set the

sun and moon on their paths. He gave a place to
everything on earth. From that time on, fish, turtles,
and whales swam in the ocean, birds flew in the
sky, and people lived on the land."

After he finished, Claudine was silent for a time.
Then she said, "I guess the gods needed light to
see with—but I feel sorry for the octopus!"

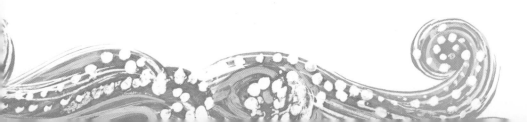

Blood and bones

"Tomás?"

Juanita poked her nose into her big brother's room. "Tomás," she asked, "is it true that no one but Indians used to live here in Mexico City?" Her brother was studying the history of Mexico in college. She knew he would be able to tell her.

Tomás grinned. "That's right. Mexico City was once the capital of the Aztec Empire."

"What were the Aztecs like?" asked Juanita.

"Very different from us," Tomás told her. "For one thing, they used to kill people on special days."

"Why did they do that?" Juanita gasped.

"Well, to understand why, you have to know the Aztec story of how the world began," said Tomás.

"The Aztecs believed that long, long ago, when there
was nothing but darkness, there was one great god
named Ometeotl, who was all alone. But then
Ometeotl gave birth to four other gods, and they
made the world."

"Did they make people?" Juanita asked.

"Not right away," answered Tomás. "First they got
into a fight that lasted a long time. The god named
Tezcatlipoca had made himself into the sun. He
was ruling the world, which was filled with giants
that the gods had made. But the god Quetzalcoatl hit
Tezcatlipoca with a club and knocked him into the
ocean! In anger, Tezcatlipoca turned himself into
a jaguar and ate all the giants!

"Then Quetzalcoatl turned himself into the sun,
made people, and began to rule the world. But

Tezcatlipoca, the jaguar, struck Quetzalcoatl with his paw and knocked him out of the sky. Then a great wind blew across the world. It tore up all the trees and killed most of the people, except for a few who were turned into monkeys. That's how monkeys came to be.

"Next, the god Tlaloc became the sun. But Quetzalcoatl sent a rain of fire down upon the earth. All the people that Tlaloc had made were killed or turned into birds. That's how birds came to be.

"Then the goddess Chalchiuhtlicue became the sun. But Tezcatlipoca made it rain so hard that the sky, which was made of water, fell down and covered the earth. All the people either drowned or became fish. That's how fish came to be.

"Now there was no land. There were no people. The sky covered everything. So Tezcatlipoca and Quetzalcoatl stopped their quarrel and lifted the sky back into place.

"Then Quetzalcoatl went to the land of the dead, where the bones of many people lay. He tricked Mictlantecuhtli, the god of the dead, into letting him take some of the bones back into the world. He took blood from his own body and let it drip onto the bones. The bones became live people, the Aztecs.

"Quetzalcoatl taught the Aztecs how to grow corn and how to weave cotton. He taught them about the stars and how to tell time. He was their favorite god. And because he had shed his blood to give them life, the Aztecs believed in giving blood back to him to show their gratitude. That's why they killed people on those special days."

Juanita nodded. "I understand," she said. "But I don't think it was very nice of them!"

The chain from heaven

Afunjo knew that his father was an anthropologist—
but he didn't know what that was. He knew that
his father spent lots of time at the museum, in the
town of Ife. And he knew his father often went to the
villages near the forest to talk with old people
whose skins were as wrinkled as raisins. But why?

Finally, Afunjo's curiosity got the best of him.

"What," he asked, "does an anthropologist do?"

"An anthropologist studies the way people live," his father told him. "He studies their customs and beliefs and the stories they tell. That's what I'm doing right now—collecting stories."

"What kind of stories?" asked Afunjo.

"The stories of our own people, the Yoruba, who live here in Nigeria," his father said. "Many of the old stories have been forgotten by everyone but our old people. The museum wants to be sure that all the stories are written down and kept, so that none will be lost."

"Tell me one of the stories," said Afunjo.

His father chuckled. "All right. I'll tell you the Yoruba story of how the world began.

"Long ago, there was nothing but a great, silent ocean that filled the sky. Above the ocean, the Great God, the Chief of Heaven, sat and thought about things.

"Finally, the Great God reached into himself and brought out a son whose name was Odudua. 'Go down to the ocean that fills the sky and put a world upon it,' the Great God said to his son.

"Odudua fastened a chain to heaven, and let it hang down so that its end reached to the ocean. Carrying a bowl of sand and a chicken, he climbed down the chain. He poured the sand out of the bowl onto the water. Lo! instead of sinking, the sand made a pile upon the water!

"Odudua placed the chicken upon the pile of sand. The chicken began to scratch the sand with its feet, spreading the sand out upon the water. Odudua covered the sand with trees and grass, and there was the world, all new and shining.

"Then Odudua brought the Yoruba people down from heaven and built the city of Ife for them to live in. He ruled them as their king, and his children became the kings, queens, and chiefs of all the towns and villages of Yorubaland."

Afunjo's father leaned back and smiled. "And that's only one of the many wonderful stories from the days of long ago, when our people had one of the richest and greatest kingdoms in all Africa."

The cloud in space

When Rick's uncle came for his usual Sunday visit, Rick was waiting for him at the door. Uncle Frank was a scientist—an astronomer—and Rick had an important question to ask him.

"Uncle Frank, can you tell me how the world began?"

His uncle sat down and lit his pipe. "Well," he said, "I can tell you how scientists think it began.

"We know that stars explode. We think that when they do, they give off huge clouds of gas and dust. This gas and dust is made up of many chemicals. There are clouds like this floating in space right now.

"Our solar system—the Sun, the Earth, and the other eight planets—was formed billions of years ago. We think it was made of clouds of gas and dust from the explosion of several stars. Gravity, the force that pulls things toward each other, pulled the different clouds of gas and dust together until there was one big cloud, hundreds of millions of miles wide.

"The cloud was probably spinning around, as all things in space do. The spinning, and the pull of gravity, made the cloud take the shape of a huge disk, like a wheel. Gravity pulled the lighter bits of gas and dust into a huge blob in the middle of the disk. This was the beginning of the Sun. Heavier bits of gas and dust formed smaller blobs that circled the big blob. One of these smaller blobs was the beginning of the Earth."

"How did the Earth get hard if it was just gas and dust?" Rick asked. "And where did the oceans and the plants and the animals come from?"

"Whoa!" cried Uncle Frank. "One thing at a time." He took a puff on his pipe and then went on. "When

things in space bump together, they make heat.
The gravity of the blob that became Earth kept pulling
more and more material to itself. All that stuff
crashing into the blob, probably every second for
millions of years, made a lot of heat! The blob got so
hot it became a glowing, molten ball.

"When the blob had pulled in all the material that
was around it, it began to cool. There were tiny bits of
iron and other hard stuff in the dust. When the
Earth cooled, this stuff got hard again. The outside

of the Earth became a hard crust. The inside
was still soft, but it was slowly cooling. Actually, it's
still cooling. Even now, the center of the Earth is
very hot and soft.

"As the Earth cooled, it gave off water vapor—
steam. When it grew cooler, the steam turned to water
and filled up all the cracks and valleys on the earth's
surface. That's how the rivers and oceans were made.

"The Earth was still hot, so the water was warm and
steamy. It was full of chemicals, too. And things

were happening to it. Rays from space were going into it, lightning was striking it, and volcanoes were pouring hot rocks into it. All these things made the chemicals join together, change, and break apart, over and over again. Scientists think that, finally, some of the chemicals formed a tiny living thing. This thing moved by itself. It took in chemicals from the water and grew. And when it grew big enough, it split into two living things that moved and ate and grew and split again.

"Millions of years passed and the oceans filled up with these tiny things. Some of them still ate chemicals, and some of them ate each other. But some of them changed and became able to make their own food. These were the first plants.

"Millions more years passed and there were more changes. Some of the things had joined together to become bigger and different things. By about 600 million years ago many different kinds of plants and animals lived in the water.

"As time passed, there were more changes. Fish appeared. Then, some kinds of fish became amphibians and came onto the land. Some of the amphibians changed into reptiles. Later, some of the reptiles changed into birds and some into mammals. And scientists think that, finally, one kind of mammal became human beings. Of course, all this took hundreds of millions of years to happen."

His pipe had gone out and he stopped to light it. Then he said, "So that's the story of the Earth according to science, Rick. Part of it we're sure about, and part of it is guesswork. And, of course, some people think we're wrong about all of it. But it certainly is a wonderful and exciting story, isn't it?"

A family scene from 2,000 years ago,
done by an unknown Greek sculptor.

Brothers and Sisters, Moms and Dads

What is a family?

To the ancient Greeks, it was a mother, father, and their children, living together in the same house. That's what the word "family" has meant to many people for thousands of years. That's what it means to many of us throughout the world today.

But there are other kinds of families, and other ways of family life. There are families in which parents and their children do not live together. There are families in which a child can have six or seven mothers and fathers, and dozens of brothers and sisters! There are families that live in the same house with as many as fifty other families.

But every kind of family shares some things with every other kind. Every kind of family is a group of people who mean much to each other, who do things together, and who share a way of life.

In that way, even the most different kinds of families are very much alike.

An Israeli family has a birthday party.

Canada

The family is the center of Eskimo life.
Eskimos love children and seldom punish them.

The smallest kind of family

Eskimos in northern Canada live in a world of terrible, freezing cold. They dress in furry clothes made of animal skins. They may eat whale fat, bear meat, and seal meat. But Eskimo families aren't very different from most families in Canada, the United States, or Europe.

An Eskimo family is usually the smallest kind of family—just a father, mother, and one or two children. And, usually, each little family lives in its own house. In the past, an Eskimo family's house was a snow igloo or a tent made of animal skins. But today, most Canadian Eskimo families live in modern, heated houses that were built for them by the government.

An Eskimo father goes to work each day, just like most fathers. Some Eskimos now work for mining or transportation companies. But many Eskimo fathers still hunt and fish to provide their families with food and clothing.

An Eskimo mother does what most mothers do. She takes care of the house and children. She makes new clothes and mends old ones.

An Eskimo family is like most little families around the world. The father goes to work. The mother stays home to care for the house and children. And the children play, just as children do everywhere.

Canada

Eskimo families follow old and new ways of life. Most of them now live in heated houses. The father may hunt seals, but with a rifle instead of a harpoon. When he gets home, his wife will use the sealskin to make clothes for their children.

Israel

This Israeli family celebrates a birthday.
They live on a big farm called a *kibbutz*.

Part-time families

On a *kibbutz* in Israel, parents and children do not
live together. The parents stay in a house for
grown-ups. The children stay in a house for children.
And babies stay in a house for babies!

A *kibbutz* is a kind of big farm. There are a number
of these farms in Israel, and many families live on
each one. Each *kibbutz* is owned by all the families
that live on it.

During the day, the children of a *kibbutz* go to
school and the grown-ups work. The children and
teachers eat lunch in school. The grown-ups eat lunch
in a big dining hall. In the evening, the children eat
with their parents in the dining hall. Then they spend
most of the evening together.

But when it is time to go to bed, the children go
back to the children's house to sleep. Their parents
usually go with them, to say good night. Then the
parents go back to the grown-ups' house to sleep.

The children on a *kibbutz* are well-cared for. Women look after the children in the children's house. Nurses take care of the babies in the babies' house.

On Saturdays, parents usually go to the children's house to get their children. If they have a baby, they get it from the babies' house. Then the whole family spends the day together.

On a *kibbutz,* parents live in a house for grown-ups. Their children live in a separate house, with all the other children.

Israel

Malaysia

This Dyak family lives in a house they share with many other families.

Many families—one house

In most villages around the world, you'll find lots of houses. But on the island of Borneo, a Dyak village may have only one house! That's because the house is a village all by itself!

A Dyak house, called a longhouse, may be a block long. And it may be the home for as many as 50 families. Sometimes these families are all related to one another. Each family has its own sleeping room and place to work. The rest of the house is one enormous room, which the families share. There is also a porch on one side of the house.

In most parts of the world, a family has its own house or apartment. And father is usually the head of the house. Naturally, a house as big as a Dyak longhouse needs a head, too. But Dyak families choose who will be the head of the house. The families in a longhouse get together and elect him.

During the day, almost everyone in the longhouse

does some kind of job. The men and older boys hunt, fish, or mend tools. Women work on the longhouse farm, or make baskets, clothes, and blankets. Children gather food for the pigs and chickens. But at night, everyone takes it easy. The families eat together. Then the big room of the longhouse becomes filled with the sounds of music, dancing, and laughter until bedtime.

Malaysia

A Dyak longhouse is really a whole village in which many families live. The little houses in back are where the families cook their food.

Norway

When grandparents, parents, and children live
together, they do most things together, too.

Four parents to a family

> *"Over the river and through the woods,*
> *To grandfather's house we go;*
> *The horse knows the way to carry the sleigh*
> *Through the white and drifted snow."*

That's part of an old American song about a happy
Thanksgiving Day visit to grandpa and grandma's
house. In many places, such a visit is a big event.
Grandchildren and grandparents often live far apart.
They may see one another only at special times.

But in some places, children, parents, and
grandparents often live together. They would think it
strange to live far apart.

On many farms in Norway there are two houses. The
grandparents live in one house. Their son and his
wife and children, or their daughter and her husband
and children, live in the other house. They all
share a happy life together on the farm.

In Japan, grandparents often live with their oldest

son and his family. Everyone is glad to have them in the house. When a new baby comes, the grandmother takes charge of the next littlest child. This leaves the mother free to care for the baby. The grandmother and the child she takes care of become very close. This child is often known as "grandmother's child."

On many Norwegian farms, the grandparents have a house close to their son's house. This makes it easy for them to visit their grandchildren.

Norway

Ghana

An Ashanti family has a meal in the mother's
house. The father lives in another house.

The biggest family of all

How would you like to have many mothers, many
fathers, and lots of brothers and sisters? Impossible?
Not if you're an Ashanti child of Ghana, in Africa.

Amfana is an Ashanti boy. He lives in a big house,
with his mother and his mother's mother. His mother's
brothers live here, too. And so do his mother's
sisters and all their children.

Amfana calls all the women in this house "mother."
So he has many "mothers." He calls all the children in
this house "brother" or "sister." So Amfana has lots
of "brothers" and "sisters."

But what about Amfana's father? Well, the father
lives in another house—with *his* mother. The father's
brothers live in this house, too. So do the father's
sisters and all their children. Amfana calls all the
grown-ups in this house "father"—even his father's
sisters! He calls the children in this house "brother"
or "sister." So he has more "brothers" and "sisters."

All Ashanti children live with their mothers—even after they are grown-up and married. But the children see their fathers all the time.

Amfana spends part of each day with his father. Sometimes, he and his mother stay with the father in his house. So Amfana not only has many mothers, many fathers, and lots of brothers and sisters—he also has two houses to live in!

Ghana

Ashanti houses are built in the shape of a hollow square, with a yard in the middle. Children, even after they are married, live with the mother's family.

A new baby in the family

The arrival of a baby is a happy, busy time for a family. Many things have to be done for the new little one. In most parts of the world, there are special ceremonies connected with the birth of a child.

Many Christian families have a ceremony called baptism. A short time after a baby is born, the parents take it to church. Here, a priest or minister puts water on the baby's head and says prayers. The baby is also given its full name. The ceremony shows that the baby is now a member of the Christian faith.

In Japan, many parents belong to the Shinto religion.

Throughout the world, most Christian babies are baptized soon after birth. This ceremony makes the baby a member of a church.

Mexico

So a month after a baby is born, the mother takes it to a Shinto shrine. Here the mother "shows" her baby to the gods and gives thanks that it is alive.

Some people have ceremonies to protect babies from danger and disease. In Swaziland, in Africa, the people burn hair and pieces of hide from wild animals. The baby is held in the smoke. They believe this will protect the child from wild animals all its life.

And in Brazil, Tchikrin Indian parents tie bands of red cloth around their baby's wrists, ankles, and knees, and paint its body red. They believe that this will help the baby grow strong because, to them, red is the color of health and strength.

Japan

In Japan, mothers take their babies to Shinto shrines to give thanks that they are alive.

Growing up

The house is gaily decorated. The guests are arriving. It is the day of *samarttiya kalyanam*. This is the day when a Tamil girl becomes a woman—at about the age of 13.

Before the ceremony, the girl dresses in her everyday clothes—a blouse and skirt, or a kind of dress called a sarong. After all the guests arrive, the girl is taken to the yard behind the house. There, a special platform called a pandal has been built. She kneels, and an older, married woman pours water over her from five brass pots.

Then a Hindu priest, who was praying while the girl was being bathed, gives her a sari. This is a beautiful kind of robe that is worn only by grown-up women. The girl goes into the house and puts on the sari and gold jewelry. For the first time in her life she is dressed as a grown woman. Then she goes back outside.

The girl's mother and sisters now take specially prepared plates of sweet foods with candles stuck into them. They wave these around the girl's head, to attract evil spirits from the girl to the food and lights. Then the girl is taken into the house. The guests give her presents and congratulate her. Now she is a woman!

All over the world there are special ceremonies that mark the end of childhood for both boys and girls. Some are joyful. Some are sober and serious. Some are scary and painful. But they're all very important to the boys and girls who take part in them. After the ceremonies, their lives change. They are no longer children. They must take on new tasks. They must learn to conduct themselves as men and women.

Ceylon

Candles, placed in a dish of food, are waved before a Tamil girl during the ceremony that marks the end of her childhood.

United States

When a Jewish boy is about 13, he has a Bar Mitzvah. This ceremony marks his entry into manhood. He must read from holy books and answer questions about his religion.

Wedding ways

One of the most important events in the life of a young man and woman is when they get married. People in different parts of the world have many different ways of getting married. Some weddings are very simple. Some are very fancy.

When a Dorze man of Ethiopia wants to be married, his friends "kidnap" his girl for him. She pretends to be afraid. But she really knows when she's going to be kidnaped. She wants to be married, too.

An Arab bride rides to the wedding tent on a camel. She is hidden under a big cloth. The camel is led around the tent seven times, then the bride goes in. Meanwhile, the groom pretends to run away! But his friends catch him and bring him to the tent.

For a Shinto wedding in Japan, most brides wear beautiful kimonos and cover their faces with white powder. During the ceremony, the bride and groom must take nine sips of rice wine together.

Ethiopia

Before a Dorze wedding, the groom's friends pretend to kidnap the bride. She acts angry and afraid, but she isn't really. She is carried to the groom's home—for a party.

Tunisia

Escorted by musicians, a
well-hidden Arab bride rides to
the wedding tent on a camel.

Japan

At most Shinto weddings, the
bride wears a traditional kimono,
and white powder on her face.

West Germany

A German bride and groom ride off in an
old-fashioned horse-drawn carriage.

United States

In most countries, people who have died are buried in the ground with a special ceremony.

A death in the family

It's a sad time when someone in the family dies. Everywhere in the world there are ceremonies that are ways of saying good-by to someone who has died.

In many parts of the world, when people die their bodies are buried in the ground. In most of North America and Europe, a dead person's body is dressed in good clothes and put into a box called a coffin. Often, there is a religious ceremony for the dead person at a church or synagogue. Then the coffin is taken to a cemetery. The dead person's family and friends watch as the coffin is lowered into the ground.

In countries where people are poor or wood is scarce, coffins are usually not used. The dead person's body is simply wrapped in a clean sheet and buried.

In Indonesia, India, Ceylon, and some other Asian countries, the bodies of people who belong to the Hindu religion are usually burned instead of buried. In India, the dead person's body is put on a pile of wood, together with offerings of flowers, leaves, and butter. Then, one of the members of the family— usually the oldest son—sets fire to the wood with a torch. Sometimes the ashes are put into a jar and kept until a member of the family can make a trip to the holy Ganges River. The ashes are then thrown into the river.

In North America and Europe, people often wear black clothes or black armbands when a member of their family dies. But in India, China, and some other countries, people often wear white clothes when someone they love has died.

Indonesia

When a Hindu dies, the body is burned. On the island of Bali, the dead person is burned on a decorated platform, covered with flowers. Sometimes a statue of a cow, which is a sacred animal, is also on the platform.

Lefevre

Zimmer

Schmidt

Dumont

Family names

Is your last name—your family name—*Smith?* Then, long ago, you had an ancestor who made things out of metal. Is your family name *Fields?* Then, long ago, you had an ancestor who lived near fields. Is your family name *Nelson?* Then, long ago, you had an ancestor whose father's name was Nels.

People didn't always have last names. So why do we have them now? There are many different reasons. In Europe, for example, last names only became common about 800 years ago. Kings and other nobles took last names to set themselves apart from the common people. It was their way of saying, "I'm better than you are." It wasn't long, however, before everyone began to take last names.

Every family name is a word that means something. All family names started out the same way. Long ago the names were words that told what kind of work a man did, or where he lived, or what his father's name was. And sometimes they were simply names of things.

The German family name *Zimmerman* means "a carpenter." The French family name *Dumont* means "of the mountain." The Russian family name *Ivanoff* means "John's son." The Italian family name Fiore means "*flower.*"

Wan *Ingolfsson* *an* *Ivanoff* *Nelson*

Family names have the same meaning in any language. Of course, they are not spelled the same. And they do not sound the same. But the meaning is the same. *Smith*, which means "metalworker," is the most common name in English. It is also a common name in other languages. If you are German, it is *Schmidt*. If you are French, it is *Lefevre*. If you are Italian, it is *Farraro*.

In most parts of the world, when a woman marries, she takes her husband's last name. When children are born, they take their father's last name. Everyone in the family has the same last name. That's why last names are called family names.

But in Iceland, everyone in a family has a different last name. Icelandic people take their father's first name as their last name. Boys add "son" to their father's name. Girls add "dottir." And when girls marry, they keep their last names.

Suppose Jon Ingolfsson marries a girl named Thora Haldorsdottir. If they have a son, his last name will be Jonsson. If they have a daughter, her last name will be Jonsdottir.

Family names aren't always *last* names. In China, a boy who is born into the Wan family, and named Lung, is called Wan Lung. In China, the family name is first.

Ivan Dhan Theod

Sean Maria

The word that means you

When a baby is born, its family gives it an important gift—its first name.

There are many reasons why parents give their children certain names. You may be named after one of your parents, or another relative. You may have a saint's name. Your given name may even be a family name. Or perhaps you are named for a famous person, place, or event.

The Pilgrims sailed from England to America more than 300 years ago. A number of children were born during the voyage. One of them was named *Oceanus*. Can you guess why?

In Greece, first names are so important that people celebrate name days instead of birthdays. Every person is named after a saint, and each saint has a special day. Greeks celebrate their name day on the day of the saint for whom they are named.

People have probably always had names. Long ago, people had only one name. Many people believed that their names were magical. If you knew someone's name, you had power over him. So people kept their names secret. Instead of their real names, they used nicknames or false names. Even today, people in some parts of the world keep their first names secret. One

Abdullah *Thomas* *ore* *Kuma* *Iahaja*

of the most precious gifts a Navaho Indian can
give someone is to tell them his or her secret name.

Most first names have a meaning. The English name
John comes from the Hebrew and means "gift of God."
Theodore, from the Greek, has the same meaning. The
English name *Thomas* means "twin." The Japanese
name *Ichiko* means "number one child." The name
Kuma means "younger" in the language of the Ashanti
people of Ghana. The Arab name *Abdullah* means
"servant of God." The East Indian name *Dhan* means
"little rice plant."

In Iceland, first names are more important than last
names. A person here is properly called by his or her
first name, even though everyone has a last name. For
this reason, Icelanders are listed in the telephone
book by their first names, not their last names.

Many names that sound different in different
languages are really all the same name. The Russian
Ivan, the Spanish *Juan,* the Turkish *Iahaja,* the
German *Johann,* the Irish *Sean,* and the Czech *Jan* are
all the same as the English *John.* The French *Marie,*
the Irish *Moira,* the Turkish *Miriem,* and the Italian
Maria are all the same as the English *Mary.*

It does not really matter what a name means. It
does not matter how many other people may have it.
Your name means *you* wherever you live.

A colonial American kitchen.

Fingers and Forks

Have you ever eaten a hush-puppy? Did you ever taste toad-in-the-hole? Do you think you'd like to try baked snails—or boiled octopus—or frozen fish eyes?

Every one of these foods is popular in some part of the world. Two of them, toad-in-the-hole and hush-puppy, are really just funny names that have been given to certain foods. The others may seem strange, but many people enjoy them—and you might, too, if you tried them!

We love to eat, and people in every part of the world have their favorite foods. Some foods are plain, some are fancy, some are spicy, some are sweet. Some foods are baked, some are boiled, some are fried. Some foods are eaten with forks, some with spoons, and some with fingers. Some foods we love and some seem awful. And some foods are so good they have been adopted by people all over the world.

English children enjoy a traditional snack of fish and chips.

Rare, medium, or well done

How you like your meat done is mostly a matter of personal taste. But where you grow up can have a lot to do with the kind of meat you like best.

The United States and Argentina raise a lot of cattle. So the people eat large amounts of beef. China raises more hogs than any other country. So the Chinese eat lots of pork. New Zealand raises a great many sheep. And, not surprisingly, New Zealanders like lamb.

What you believe has a great deal to do with the kind of meat you eat—or even if you eat meat at all. In Pakistan, most of the people are Moslems. Like Orthodox Jews, Moslems do not eat pork. But they do enjoy shish kebab—bits of lamb roasted on a stick with slices of tomato, pepper, and onion. Buddhists do not eat meat. Their beliefs forbid them to kill animals.

Spain

Spanish butcher shops sell mostly goat, pork, lamb, rabbit, and chicken.

United States

Barbecues are popular on Texas ranches. Beef and other meats are roasted over an open fire.

Pakistan

A boy sells shish kebab—bits of lamb roasted on a stick with slices of tomato, pepper, and onion. This Armenian dish is popular in many countries.

France

Oysters are gathered at low tide in shallow water. They are often eaten raw.

United States

Fresh crabs and lobsters can be bought at the Farmers Market in Los Angeles.

Food from the water

You're at a smorgasbord—a big Scandinavian meal—
in Sweden. A long table is filled with all kinds of fish,
meat, and other food. You can take as much as you
want. You can go back for seconds and thirds!
But on your first trip, you should take *only* fish. And
there's plenty of that—pickled herring, smoked salmon,
baked halibut, and more. People in Sweden eat lots
of seafood prepared in many different ways.

You're at a dinner in Japan. You are given a bowl
with some thin, cold slices of something pink in it.
You try a slice. It's good! You ask your host what it
is. He smiles and tells you it's sashimi—raw fish.
People in Japan eat lots of seafood prepared in many
different ways.

In fact, almost everyone enjoys food that comes from
the water. Not only fish, but oysters, clams, crabs,
lobsters, shrimps—practically everything that swims.

Eat your vegetables

When an American mother says to her children, "Eat your vegetables," she probably means spinach, or string beans, or peas. These are common vegetables in North America. But in other parts of the world, when a mother says, "Eat your vegetables," she may mean something quite different.

In Java, people enjoy *asinam*, a vegetable dish made of mustard leaves, bean sprouts, bean paste, radishes, and peanuts. In China, a very popular vegetable is lotus roots—the root of a lotus flower. The Chinese slice the roots and eat them as a salad. The sliced roots look like round pieces of Swiss cheese.

People mostly eat the kinds of plants that grow best in the place where they live. And many kinds of plants will grow only in certain places. So there are often very different plants in different parts of the world. For example, olives need a hot, dry climate. There are no olives in hot, wet Indonesia. But there are plenty of them in sunny, dry Italy. The people make oil from them, and eat them green, ripe, stuffed, and pickled.

South Africa

An African woman cooks squash in her sunny, outdoor kitchen.

Spain

Bright red, yellow, and green
fruits and vegetables draw
shoppers to a Spanish market.

Iran

A small, furry donkey carries
a large load of his master's
goods to an outdoor market.

Reindeer milk and yak butter

"Milk comes from the reindeer. Everyone knows that." Paavo pushed back his brightly colored hat to scratch his head. "At least I *thought* everyone knew that," he said. "My father has the finest herd of reindeer in all Lapland. We use their hides for tents and for clothes. We eat their strong-tasting meat. And their rich milk makes the best butter and cheese."

Vashni smiled shyly and pulled her beautiful sari up around her shoulders. "I am sorry to tell you, but milk comes from the water buffalo. In my village in India, every family drinks the milk of the buffalo."

"Whoever heard of drinking buffalo milk?" laughed George. "Milk comes from cows. On our farm in Wisconsin, we have more than 300 milk cows. And each cow gives about 4,000 quarts of milk a year!"

"How can what you say be true?" asked Abdul. "All the children of my tribe drink the milk of the camel. Camels have very bad tempers, but very good milk. It is rich and thick and makes good cheese. Ask any Arab in Saudi Arabia. What I tell you is so."

"Why ask an Arab? I *know* where milk comes from!" shouted Orestes. "It is a fact that milk comes from a goat. And if you want good cheese, try some Greek *feta*. My mother makes it from goat's milk."

Jamal shook his head in wonder. "Never before have I heard a yak called by so many different names." He looked at his friends, a happy smile on his broad face. "But I joke. Each of you is right. All these animals give milk. And each of you is wrong, for no milk is as good as the milk of the yak. And as for yak butter—well, that is the best. Come with me to Tibet and you will find out where milk comes from!"

Sweden

Some Lapps, a people who live
in northern Europe, still use
reindeer milk to make cheese.

France

Breakfast may mean a trip to the bakery for fresh bread.

Iran

Bread baked in thin, flat sheets hangs on display outside an Iranian bakery.

The first man-made food

It is the oldest of all foods made by man. It comes in all shapes and sizes. It is called "the staff of life." More people eat it than any other kind of food. In the United States, it's name is a slang term for money. What is it?

If you haven't guessed, it's—bread!

The early breads were hard and flat. They were made by mixing ground grain and water. The Egyptians were the first to make bread that is soft and light and filled with air. They also made the first ovens, because they needed a different way to bake the larger mass of dough used for this new kind of bread.

People use different grains to make bread. Each grain gives it a different color and taste. And, of course, people have different names for bread.

In the Southwestern United States, Mexico, and Central and South America, you can enjoy flat corn-meal cakes called tortillas. In the Middle East, try Arab *pita*, which is made from wheat. In India, you can have flat wheat cakes called chapatties. And, if you are in France, buy a long loaf of *pain*, which is French for bread.

Jordan

Bedouins enjoy *pita*, a flat bread made from wheat.

Colombia

A young girl in Colombia prepares a thin, corn-meal pancake called a tortilla, which people in her country use like bread.

Spain

A baker decorates a fancy dessert.
Made of ground almonds and sugar,
it's filled with dried fruits.

In Vermont, "sugaring off" means
pouring maple syrup on snow and
eating it with doughnuts and pickles.

United States

What's for dessert?

Do you have a "sweet tooth"? You do if you like yummy, mouth-watering desserts and other kinds of sweets.

Marzipan is a sweet made of ground almonds and sugar. It is a favorite for fancy desserts because it can be colored and shaped. If you want a scary dessert, you might find a Spanish baker who will make you a marzipan dragon.

Have you ever been to a "sugaring off" party in Vermont? Here, the sap of the maple trees is collected in late winter. When the sap is boiled to make maple syrup, the neighbors come to help. And, of course, there's a party. Maple syrup is poured on the snow and eaten—topped off with doughnuts and pickles!

Some basic foods are used to make fine candies and tasty desserts. Children in Mexico love sweet potato candy. In the Philippines, *comote-cues*, a dessert made from sweet potatoes, is a favorite. In Burma, children buy *pauk pauk mow*, bits of candy made of puffed rice. And Indonesians like *lemang*, a dessert of rice baked in banana leaves.

Mexico

Children in Mexico love sweet potato candy.

Indonesia

A market place in Sumatra sells *lemang*, a dessert of rice baked in banana leaves.

China

A family living on a junk cooks
a meal of meat and vegetables
over a charcoal fire built in
a tin container.

What's cooking?

In China, Wang Kow watches his mother make
dinner. She pours some peanut oil into a big, round,
metal bowl called a *wok*. The *wok* sits on top of a small
charcoal stove. As the oil gets hot, it begins to hiss.
Quickly she puts meat, bean sprouts, onions, and pea
pods into the oil. They begin to crackle crisply. This
kind of cooking, in hot oil, is called frying.

On the island of Cyprus, Pietro's mother is making
bread. She shares a big, dome-shaped oven with many
other women. Glowing coals fill the bottom of the oven.
Loaves of bread are put on shelves above the coals.
This kind of cooking is called baking.

On the island of Sicily, Lucca watches his brother
cook a freshly caught octopus by putting it in boiling
water. This kind of cooking is called boiling.

There are other kinds of cooking, too. Roasting is
very much like baking. Broiling is done by putting food
on a rack over heat. Throughout the world, people
have many ways of cooking all the foods they eat.

Cyprus

These women on the island of Cyprus
share an oven to bake their bread.

On a seashore in Sicily, boys
gather for a meal of boiled octopus.

Italy

Japan

A schoolboy uses chopsticks to eat a lunch of rice balls.

The members of this Arab family sit in a circle to spoon their food from the same bowl.

Tunisia

When do we eat?

Grrrr. Your stomach is growling. You're hungry. It's long past the time you usually eat. But when do you eat? And how often? And how?

The answers to these questions depend on where you live. When, how often, and how we eat is a matter of custom. And custom is just a way of doing something —a way we have decided is best for us.

People in most Western countries eat three times a day. But England is a Western country, and the English are used to an extra meal. They call it tea, or tiffin, and have it in the late afternoon. And Norwegians usually eat four meals—but many farm families in Norway have five meals a day.

Most Americans and Europeans eat from individual plates and use a knife, fork, and spoon. But when having a snack, fingers are in order. When the English stop for some fish and chips— fried fish and French fried potatoes— they eat with their fingers.

Most Arab families eat from a common, central bowl. They eat only with the right hand, whether they use fingers or spoons. The left hand is considered unclean. Japanese and Chinese pick up their food with chopsticks. They don't need knives. Their food is prepared in small pieces.

England

Fish and chips—fried fish and French fried potatoes—are a favorite in England. They are often wrapped in paper, taken out, and eaten with the fingers.

These schoolboys use their fingers to eat their lunch.

Malaysia

Seaweed, snails, and frozen fish eyes

If you were offered seaweed, or snails, or frozen fish eyes, what would you do? Would you turn up your nose in disgust? Or would you say, "Yes, thank you!"?

In Japan, seaweed is an important food. In Wales, the people like a vegetable dish called *bara laver* that is made from seaweed. And a lot of people eat seaweed without knowing it. That's because it is used to make ice cream, candy, and jellies.

Many people, but especially the French, think that snails baked in garlic sauce are very tasty. They also enjoy raw sea urchins. Eskimo children love frozen fish eyes and maggots scraped from animal skins.

People learn to like the foods they get used to. If certain foods seem strange to you, it's just because you never learned to eat them.

Thorn-covered sea urchins may not look very tasty, but many French people love them. The insides are eaten raw, usually with bread.

France

Japan

Japanese women harvest a crop of seaweed in a shallow bay. It will be dried and used for food.

Eskimos enjoy fat maggots scraped from the inside of a caribou skin.

Canada

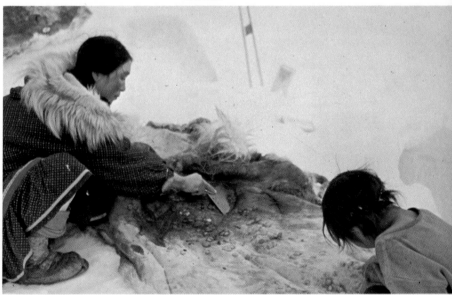

England: toad-in-the-hole

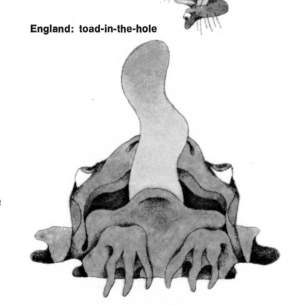

England: toad-in-the-hole

What is it?

Some of the very tastiest foods have the funniest names. Most of the time, you can't tell from the name what the food is. But these funny names do tell us that people in all parts of the world have a good sense of humor—even about something as important as food.

Can you guess what these foods are?

China: dragon's whiskers

United States: hush-puppy

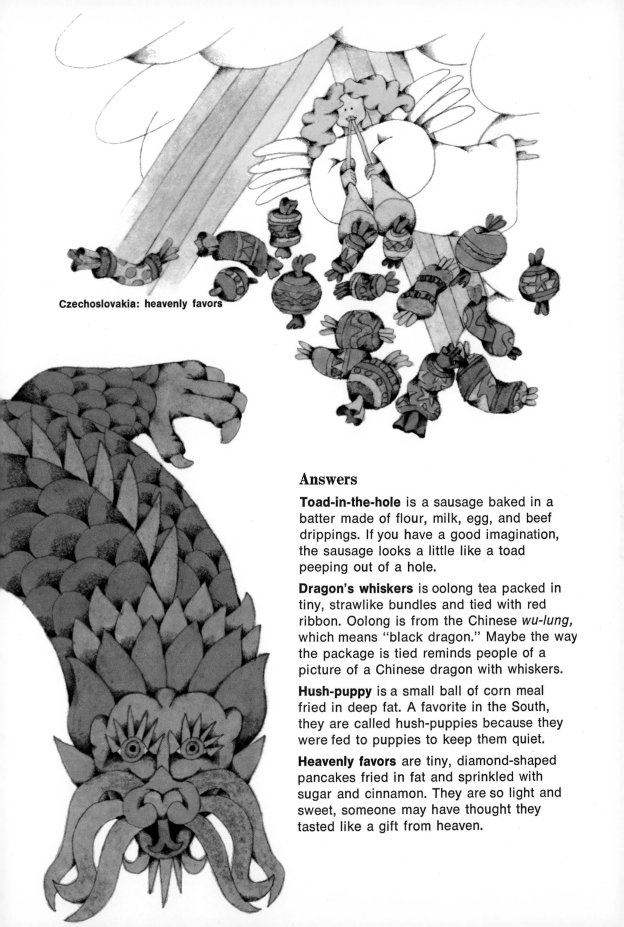

Czechoslovakia: heavenly favors

Answers

Toad-in-the-hole is a sausage baked in a batter made of flour, milk, egg, and beef drippings. If you have a good imagination, the sausage looks a little like a toad peeping out of a hole.

Dragon's whiskers is oolong tea packed in tiny, strawlike bundles and tied with red ribbon. Oolong is from the Chinese *wu-lung,* which means "black dragon." Maybe the way the package is tied reminds people of a picture of a Chinese dragon with whiskers.

Hush-puppy is a small ball of corn meal fried in deep fat. A favorite in the South, they are called hush-puppies because they were fed to puppies to keep them quiet.

Heavenly favors are tiny, diamond-shaped pancakes fried in fat and sprinkled with sugar and cinnamon. They are so light and sweet, someone may have thought they tasted like a gift from heaven.

The Blue Boy, by the English artist Thomas Gainsborough.

What Should I Wear Today?

No one knows why people first wore clothes. Or when. No one knows if the first clothing was a warm animal skin or a pretty necklace made of sea shells. But chances are that we have always worn clothes for just about the same reasons.

We wear clothes to keep ourselves warm or dry. Some of us—kings and queens, policemen and soldiers, priests and ministers—wear clothes that show who we are or what we do. And, perhaps most important of all, we wear clothes to make ourselves look nice.

The painting called "The Blue Boy," by Thomas Gainsborough, shows an English boy of 300 years ago dressed in his fanciest clothes. The clothes are decorated with lace, bows, and ruffles. He has a big feather in his hat.

We wear very different kinds of clothes now—but we still decorate them in many ways. Even people who wear hardly anything, often decorate themselves with beads, feathers, and dabs of paint.

Teen-age American girls wearing jeans decorated with embroidered designs.

Mukluks and jellabas

The land looks flat and white under a blanket of frozen snow. Glittering stars dot the coal-black sky. A bitterly cold wind moans through the icy Arctic air. Across the snow, behind a sled pulled by seven large, shaggy dogs, comes a man.

The man is an Eskimo. He is dressed in clothes made of animal skins. A hooded jacket, or parka, protects the upper part of his body. Under it the Eskimo wears still another jacket. He also wears two pairs of pants to protect his legs. The heat from his body is trapped between the two sets of clothes. This helps to keep him warm. Thick fur mittens cover his hands. And to protect his feet from the terrible cold, he wears sealskin boots called mukluks.

Half a world away, another man rides a long-legged camel across the Arabian Desert. The burning sun above him is a huge disk in a cloudless sky. The air is so hot it seems to dance as it rises from the sand.

This man is a desert Arab, a Bedouin. He wears a white linen robe that covers him from his shoulders to his ankles. The loose folds of the robe allow air to flow in and out and around his body. This helps to keep him cool. Wrapped around his head is a length of white cloth. One end of the cloth is pulled over his mouth and nose to keep out blowing sand.

Behind him, tied to the saddle, is a hooded woolen cloak called a jellaba. At night the desert sometimes gets so cold there is frost on the sand! Then the Arab will put on his jellaba to keep warm.

The Arab's clothes don't look at all like those of the Eskimo. But each man's clothing protects him from the weather in his part of the world.

Canada

Clothes made of animal skins protect this Eskimo from the terrible Arctic cold as he fishes through the ice.

Tuaregs, a fierce desert people of the Sahara, enjoy practice sword fights. Like Bedouins, they wear long robes and special head coverings that protect them from the burning desert sun.

Mali

Who needs clothes?

Deep in the Ituri Forest, in the heart of Africa, a band of Pygmies is hunting. The forest is hot and damp and dark. Water drips from the trees. For clothing, the Pygmies wear only a bit of cloth wrapped about the waist.

Thousands of miles to the east lie the Philippines. Here, in another hot, damp, and dark forest, live the Tasaday people. As they go about their daily work, they wear only little aprons made of leaves.

To the south is Australia, the huge country that is also a continent. Some of the original people, the Aborigines, still roam the vast deserts as did their fathers before them. Because the climate is hot and dry, the Aborigines often do not wear any clothes at all.

Among some people, a piece of jewelry may be all the clothing considered necessary. But if so, they wouldn't think of going out without it. In their way, they are just as modest as people who cover themselves from head to foot.

Zaire

These Bambuti Pygmies are hunting an animal in their forest home. The forest is hot and damp, so they do not need much clothing.

Australia

These Aborigine children live in a hot, dry desert. They, and their parents, often don't wear clothes. Many Aborigine children have blonde hair, but it darkens as they grow older.

Norway

Lapps love clothes that are brightly
colored and gaily decorated.

Feathers, furs, and fringes

Once upon a time, people lived in caves and did not
wear clothes. One day, a man noticed a beautiful
orange and black butterfly.

"I wish I were covered with pretty colors like that,"
said the man. "Then everyone would notice and
admire me. I would be the center of attention."

Then he had a wonderful idea. He made red and
black paint out of red clay and charcoal. He
painted red and black designs on an animal skin and
wrapped the skin around himself. All the other
cave people cried, "Look at him! Doesn't he look fine!"
Soon they were all making clothes for themselves.
Everyone wanted to look fine, too.

Of course, it probably didn't happen this way. But

it could have. People may have first worn clothes just to make themselves look nice. We still do everything we can think of to make our clothes—and ourselves—look beautiful.

We weave cloth with bold patterns and dye it with bright colors. When the cloth has been made into a robe, a suit, or a dress, we often decorate it with beads, feathers, fur, lace, or fringe.

Clothes don't need to be pretty. A plain black coat is just as warm as a bright red one. But most of us like to wear colorful clothes. What kind of clothes do you like to wear?

A shawl decorated with fringe and a derbylike hat are part of the traditional costume of many South American Indian women.

Bolivia

United States

Many teen-agers like to decorate their jeans and jackets with bright, embroidered designs.

United States

The Amish people have strict religious beliefs. Their way of dressing makes them look different from their neighbors.

Clothes tell the story

Lost! The first time out alone in a strange city and you are lost. But no matter. All you have to do is find a policeman. He'll be able to help. So off you go, confident that you'll have no trouble picking out a policeman.

Why so sure? Because policemen wear uniforms so that everyone will know them. Of course you might make a mistake and go up to a postman or a fireman. But sooner or later you'll find a policeman.

Clothes can tell us a lot. They can tell us what kind of work a person does. They can tell us that a person is a member of a particular religious group. And kings and other chiefs wear clothes that seem to say, "Look at all this finery! You can tell I'm important!"

Thailand

These Buddhist monks are easily recognized by their orange robes.

Fiji

Policemen in every country wear uniforms that show who they are.

Iran

The Shah of Iran, like other kings, wears clothes that are so rich looking that everyone knows he is someone important.

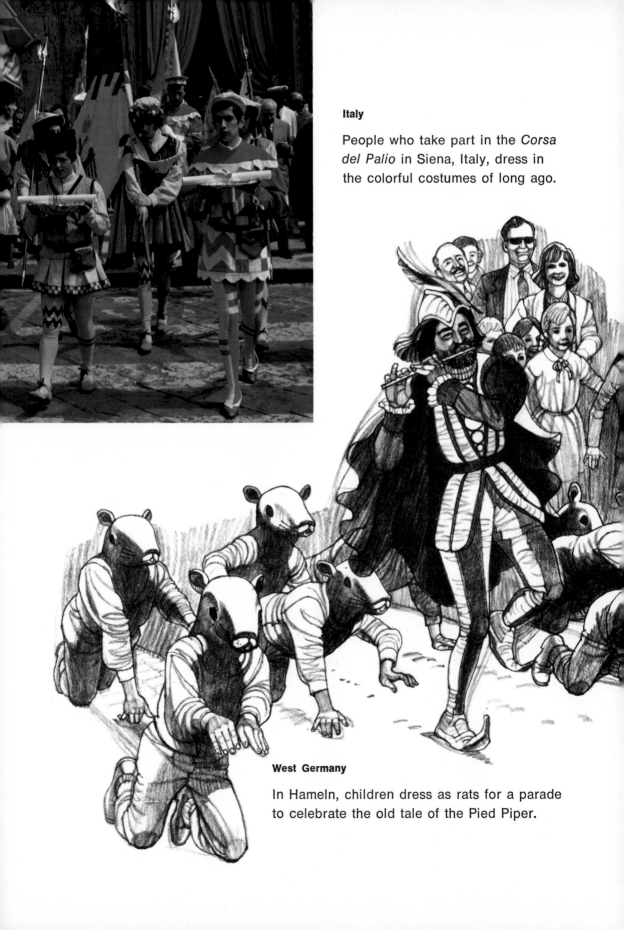

Italy

People who take part in the *Corsa del Palio* in Siena, Italy, dress in the colorful costumes of long ago.

West Germany

In Hameln, children dress as rats for a parade to celebrate the old tale of the Pied Piper.

Let's dress up!

Look! Giant rats! No—they're children dressed up as rats! And here comes the Pied Piper! You're at a festival in the city of Hameln, Germany. The people are dressed up in these costumes to celebrate the famous story of the Pied Piper of Hamelin.

Here comes a parade of knights. Look at the gaily dressed drummers and trumpeters! You're in Siena, Italy. The people are dressed up in the clothes of long ago. Once each year they put on these costumes and go to horse races known as the *Palio*.

All over the world there are special days when people put on special clothes. It seems as if all of us, everywhere, sometimes like to dress up and become someone or something different.

(continued on page 104)

United States

This Umatilla Indian from Oregon is dressed for a special tribal ceremony.

Let's dress up

(continued from page 103)

Switzerland

Just before Lent, people in Einsiedeln dress up in fantastic costumes. Then they go through the town ringing giant bells.

Bolivia

At a special time each year, many people of the town of Oruro dress up as angels and devils. These dancers are dressed as devils.

Papua New Guinea

On sing-sing day in New Guinea, men from many different tribes gather for a big celebration. They paint themselves and dress in costumes made of feathers, shells, and leaves. These men of the Asaro tribe have mud-smeared bodies and frightening masks made of mud.

Kuwait

Many Arabs wear Western work clothes instead of robes. But they keep their traditional head cloth, the kaffiyeh.

Kilts, kimonos, and kaffiyehs

Boys in the United States would laugh at the idea of wearing a skirt. But in Scotland, boys and men often wear a kind of pleated skirt called a kilt. In Japan, everyone likes to put on a beautiful robe called a kimono. And desert Arabs usually prefer to wear their traditional headdress, the kaffiyeh.

These people are all proud of their national costumes. They think them beautiful and find them comfortable. But for everyday wear, many are adopting the kind of clothes worn in the United States, Canada, and Western Europe. Even so, they often wear their traditional costumes around the house or put them on to celebrate a special holiday.

Scotland

For hundreds of years, Scottish men and boys have proudly worn a kind of skirt called a kilt.

Japan

Kimonos are beautiful robes often worn by men, women, and children in Japan.

An ancient Indian cliff dwelling in Colorado.

Let's Go to My House

The very first kind of house was a cave. It had walls that kept out harsh winds and prowling animals. It had a ceiling that kept out the rain. It had a floor on which to sit or curl up and sleep.

In time, people learned to build houses. They used whatever materials were handy. In dry places, houses were made of mud or clay. Where there was plenty of wood, people built houses of logs. On grassy plains, they built houses of dry grass. They learned to use mud and clay to stick stones together, and they made great towers of stone, such as the cliff dwellings in the Southwestern United States.

Today, many people still live in houses made of mud, or dry grass, or logs. Others live in houses made of concrete and steel. But no matter where we live, or what kind of house we live in, our houses are much like that first cave. They have walls, ceilings, and floors to protect us from rain, snow, and wind.

A modern apartment building in Canada.

An African igloo

An igloo in Africa? Oh, that's a silly idea? It would melt, you say?

Well, not necessarily. You see, "igloo" is the Eskimo word for house—any kind of house. An igloo can be made of wood, stone, mud, canvas, skins, grass—or snow. So you could have an igloo in Africa. But not a snow igloo.

In North Africa, where it is hot and dry, mud is a good building material. The Egyptians use mud bricks that have been dried in the sun. And people in the Sudan make huts with mud walls. They plaster the mud over branches.

The Southwestern United States is also hot and dry. Houses here are often made of adobe. Adobe is the Spanish name for sun-dried bricks.

Mud or adobe houses have thick walls to keep them cool. Many have flat roofs where people can eat and sleep on cool nights.

Afghanistan

Houses made of mud or stone are just right for the hot, dry climate of this Asian kingdom.

Nigeria

The city of Kano is in northern Nigeria, where it is hot and dry. The people live in mud houses. Thick walls help to keep the houses cool.

Peru

The western side of the Andes Mountains is cool and dry. Because there is little rain, the people who live here can build their houses with sun-dried bricks.

United States

Navahos live in the American Southwest. Their houses, called hogans, are built of logs covered with earth.

Water, water, everywhere

Arabs have camels, sheep, and tents. And they live in sandy deserts, right? Well, not always. In Iraq, there are Arabs who have canoes, water buffaloes, and reed houses. And they live in a big, wet marsh.

Growing in this marsh are giant reeds, often 25 feet high. The marsh dwellers build their houses with the reeds. But first, they have to make an island. To do this, they drive short, stiff bundles of reeds into water about three feet deep. The enclosed area is filled with plants to make the "ground."

Big bundles of full-length reeds are stuck into the "ground." These are the sides. The tops are bent in and tied to form an arched roof. Smaller bundles of reeds are tied across the upright bundles. Finally, this reed framework is covered with reed mats.

Iraq has little rain. But in spring, melting snow in the mountains makes the rivers overflow and flood the marshes. So each house has a platform. The family lives on it until the water goes down.

A house built on stilts stays
dry even when the water rises.

Colombia

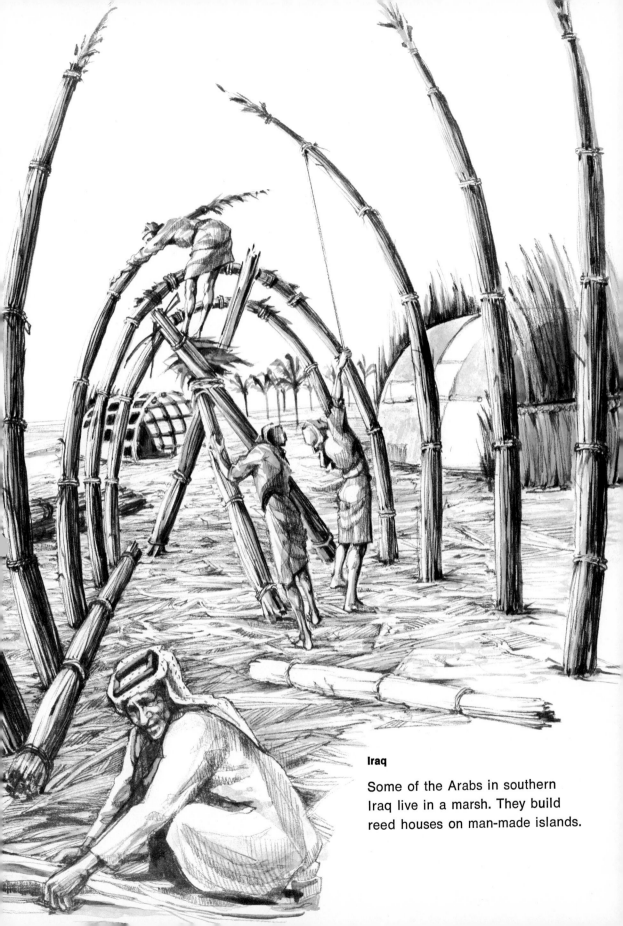

Iraq

Some of the Arabs in southern
Iraq live in a marsh. They build
reed houses on man-made islands.

United States

Playing in the snow is lots of fun. But it's also good to come into a nice warm house. A house made of wood is just right for the cold winters and cool summers in Minnesota.

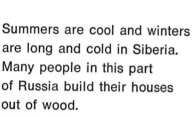

Summers are cool and winters are long and cold in Siberia. Many people in this part of Russia build their houses out of wood.

Russia

France
Stone houses withstand the
rainy climate and changing
seasons in Brittany.

A house for all seasons

It might be fun to have a house for each season.
How about a bamboo house with a thatched roof for
warm, rainy spring days? On hot, dry summer
days, a house with thick, mud walls is a cool place.
Then for brisk fall days, you could have a sod house to
keep out cool winds and chilling rains. And for
winter, a snow igloo could keep you snug and warm.

Of course, your houses wouldn't last long in such
changing weather. And building a new house every few
months would be an awful bother. So people who
live where there are changing seasons build their houses
out of materials that will last a long time.

Wood, stone, brick, and concrete stand up well under
snow, rain, wind, and sun. To keep houses warm
in winter, people put in stoves, fireplaces, and furnaces.
And windows, awnings, fans, and air conditioners
help to keep houses cool when the weather turns hot.

United States

The Pueblo Indians of the American Southwest
are famous for their apartment-house villages.
This pueblo in Taos, New Mexico, has been
lived in for nearly 300 years.

One house on top of another

Houses piled on top of one another—so high they
seem to reach the sky. Where are they? In almost
every city. They are called high-rise apartments.

A city is a place where thousands—and sometimes
millions—of people live and work. In a crowded
city, there isn't enough land for every family to have
its own house. Apartment houses—buildings with
the houses one on top of another—are the only answer.

Many modern apartment houses are 50 or more
stories high. One invention—and one alone—made
these apartment houses possible. Can you guess what
it was? If you guessed *elevator*, you are right. If it
were not for the elevator, apartment houses or office

buildings could only be a few stories high.

In the Southwestern United States, there are apartment buildings that are 300 years old. They are called pueblos—a Spanish word meaning a people or community. Some of the early pueblos were as many as five stories high. They were built so that the roofs of the lower rooms were porches for the rooms above.

When the first pueblos were built, there was plenty of land. The Indians built up for protection, not to save land. The only way to get into a pueblo was up a ladder and through a hole in the roof. When an enemy was near, the Indians just pulled up the ladders.

Several families live in each of these apartment houses built along a canal in the city of Amsterdam.

The Netherlands

Canada

Habitat, built in Montreal in 1967, looks a little like a pueblo. The roof of each unit is a terrace for the unit above.

Cave for rent

A cave can be a dark, musty, creepy place—a den
for bats, birds, and crawly things that whir and
buzz. Or a cave can be a cozy house for a family.

In southern Spain, many families live in caves. Why?
Because a cave is cool in summer and warm in
winter. The families in these caves are sheltered from
rain, wind, and cold. In fact, a cave is most of the
things a good house is supposed to be. And it doesn't
cost much to live in one of these caves.

Of course, a cave has to be fixed up before it can be
lived in. Modern cave dwellers get rid of the bats
and clean out the cave. Then they build rooms with
doors and windows. Sometimes they even bring
in electricity. Finally, they hang pictures on the walls
and put carpets on the floors.

These Spanish caves are much nicer than those the
cave men lived in thousands of years ago. If you
could choose, would you live in a cave or in an
ordinary house?

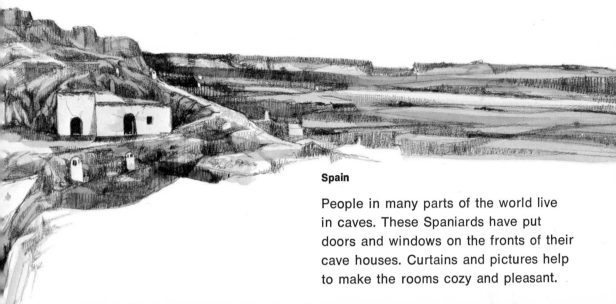

Spain

People in many parts of the world live in caves. These Spaniards have put doors and windows on the fronts of their cave houses. Curtains and pictures help to make the rooms cozy and pleasant.

We take our houses with us

Imagine moving four times a year! The reindeer herders of Lapland have to. These nomads, or wanderers, live in the far north. Their homeland stretches across Norway, Sweden, Finland, and into Russia. For Lapland isn't a land or a country—it's a region.

The Lapps depend upon reindeer for everything—food, clothing, and shelter. With every change of season, the herd must be moved to new grazing ground. And when they move, the Lapps take their houses with them.

A Lapp "house" is a cone-shaped tent, like an American Indian tepee. It is made of 12 poles covered with reindeer hides. A hole at the top lets out the smoke from the fire. The hole can be closed to keep in some heat, but it is often as cold inside as it is outside.

The ground in the tent is covered with birch twigs. There is no furniture. Everyone sleeps on the ground. Even the dogs are allowed to crowd in.

When it's time to move, the tent is taken down and packed on a sled or on the back of a reindeer. Usually there are about six families in a group, or clan. Each family owns about 300 reindeer. And some 2,000 reindeer on the move is a never-to-be-forgotten sight.

(continued on page 122)

A house on wheels is just the thing if you like to travel. Each year, more and more American families use these "mobile homes" for vacations.

United States

Norway

Lapp reindeer herders move four times a
year. Their movable "houses" are tents.

We take our houses with us

(continued from page 121)

In central Asia, between China and Russia, there is a small country called Mongolia. Some of the people here still follow their traditional nomadic way of life. These Mongolians move from pasture to pasture with their horses, sheep, goats, and yaks.

They live in a large, round tent called a yurt. A yurt has a framework of wooden poles, covered with heavy felt. It is often well furnished and is comfortable in hot and cold weather. When it's time to move, the yurt is loaded on a pack animal or in a cart.

Mongolia

Mongol herdsmen live in tents called yurts. When they are ready to move, the yurts are taken down and loaded on camels or other pack animals.

Mongolia

For thousands of years, Mongols have been famous as horsemen. Some are still wandering herdsmen who follow their animals across a rugged land.

Mongolia

Yurts look like very plain and simple shelters. But many of them are beautifully furnished and very comfortable to live in.

Riding the waves

How would you like to live in a house that bobs up and down like a cork in a bowl of water? Some families live like this because it is the only kind of house they can afford. Others find that a house on the water makes good sense or can be lots of fun.

The rivers and harbors of the Far East are crowded with houseboats called sampans. Most are about 20 feet long, with a cramped, mat-covered cabin. Many people are born and live all their lives on a sampan.

Some families in Europe live on barges. These large boats carry cargoes on the canals and rivers. While father earns a living as a barge pilot, he doesn't have to be away from his family. They come with him.

Along the Rio Negro (Black River) in Brazil, Indian families build their houses on rafts. When there are floods during the rainy season, they don't have any problem. Their raft houses rise with the water.

In the United States and Canada, many families use houseboats as vacation cottages. Others live in them all year round. For them, riding the waves is fun.

France

Barge families have very little living space.
Even a simple job, such as washing dishes,
is hard when there is not much room. But at
least the family is always together.

This ancient Egyptian tomb painting shows farmers at work more than 3,000 years ago.

The Ways We Work

The sun is shining on our backs.
In town, we shall be paid fish for our barley.

That was a song of Egyptian farmers, more than 3,000 years ago. Wall paintings in ancient tombs show these farmers at work in their fields.

People have always had to work for a living. At first they hunted and fished. Later, they learned to farm. They made most of their own clothes, tools, and furniture. They traded some of the things they made, or grew, or caught, for other things they needed. Then money was invented. As people began to work for money, they used it to buy things.

Some of us still farm and fish. But we sell much of what we grow or catch. Some of us have jobs making goods for others to buy. We are craftsmen and factory workers. Some of us have jobs helping others. We are teachers, scientists, policemen, doctors.

Year after year, we learn, we discover, we invent. As a result, we are always finding more and different kinds of work to do.

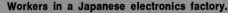

Workers in a Japanese electronics factory.

The good earth

Kazino had set out early that morning. He had driven the cattle for an hour before finding enough grass for them to feed on. Now he brushed away the flies around his eyes and squinted at the sun. It was time to round up the herd.

In the distance, he could see wild animals. He gripped his long-bladed spear tightly. It would be wise to get home before dark. At night, the wild animals might attack the cattle.

Kazino is a Masai. He lives with his tribe in a village on a reservation in Kenya, Africa. In the center of the village there is a pen where the cattle are kept at night.

Kazino's people do not hunt animals or grow crops for food. They live on meat, milk, and blood from their cattle. Without grass, the cattle would starve. Without cattle, the Masai would starve. In this way, the Masai depend on the land for a living.

Farmers, oil drillers, and lumbermen also depend on the land for a living. In Israel, many workers earn money growing, picking, and packing oranges. In Wales, miners dig for coal.

In every country in the world, people work with the riches that are found in the good earth.

Kenya

The Masai of Kenya, Africa, depend on cattle for food. The herder's job is important.

Wales

Digging coal out of the ground is hard and dirty work. These Welsh miners use donkeys to haul the loaded coal carts out of the mine.

Israel

Many Israelis pick oranges for a living. They have to climb high up in the trees to get all the fruit.

United States

Alaskan fishermen haul in the huge
traps they use to catch king crabs.

Norway

Fishermen are busiest from
January through April. Even
young boys help clean fish
and get them ready for
markets around the world.

Colombia

Goajiro Indians gather salt
from the sea. They rake the
salt into piles so that it
can dry in the sun.

Riches in the sea

When Per meets a neighbor, he usually
says, *"Godt fiske!"* instead of "Good
day!" *Godt fiske* means "good fishing" in
Norwegian. And a good catch means
a good day for all Norwegian fishermen.

For thousands of years, Norwegians
have made a living from the sea. These
fishermen are busiest from January to
April. This is when there are millions of
cod around the Lofoten Islands.

Per and his neighbors haul in tons of
cod with their nets. When they return
to the village, they clean and salt the
cod and hang them on racks to dry. Then
the cod are sold in markets around
the world.

When the fishing season is over, the
fishermen find other work. Some go
to work in factories. Others are part-time
farmers. A few work on ferries that
carry people across fiords.

Fish are not the only things in the
sea. Alaskan fishermen also catch crabs
and shrimp. The Goajiro Indians in
Colombia, South America, gather salt
from the sea. In Japan, workers
pick seaweed that can be eaten. And off
the coasts of Florida, Tunisia, Egypt,
Greece, and Turkey, divers bring
up sponges from the ocean bottom.

All these workers, and many more,
earn a living from riches in the sea.

Japan

Japanese, working on an assembly line, put
television sets together piece by piece.

Piece by piece

"We make small things in a big way." That's what
Swiss factory workers say. Watches are one of
the small things the Swiss are famous for making.
They make about half the watches in the world.

Herr Hedli works in a watch factory. The rooms are
brightly lighted and spotlessly clean. Machines
whir, click, and pump. They turn out dials, springs,
cases, and other parts of watches.

Dressed in white coats, men and women sit at long
tables. This is the assembly line. Each worker
does a little bit on each watch. Some of the workers
use magnifying glasses and tweezers. Carefully,

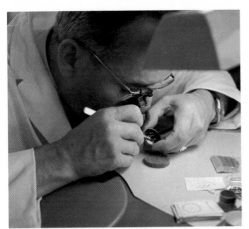

Switzerland

A Swiss watchmaker uses tweezers to insert a tiny watch part.

Spain

Workers assemble bicycle parts in a factory in Spain.

piece by piece, they put each watch together.

Herr Hedli sits near the end of the row. His job is to put in the last part of the watch—the balance wheel unit. He taps the wheel with his tweezers. The watch begins to tick.

Switzerland does not have the coal, iron, or oil that are needed for heavy industry. But Switzerland does have many skilled workers. So instead of making big things, Swiss factory workers make small, valuable items such as watches. This work takes lots of skill, but only small amounts of raw materials.

In big factories everywhere, each worker makes only a part of the whole thing. This way, more things can be made faster.

We make the whole thing

Millions of look-alike socks and shoes, pots and pans, toys and toothbrushes tumble out of machines. But before there were machines, people made things by hand. And there are still people who make things by hand.

There are few factories in the kingdom of Afghanistan, in southern Asia. But there are many craftsmen who work at home or in small shops. They make shiny copper pots, colorful wool rugs, leather goods, and cotton and wool cloth. These craftsmen make each thing by hand from start to finish. And no two things ever look exactly the same.

In every country in the world, even where there are factories, people make things by hand. Sometimes they are too poor to buy factory-made things. Sometimes, they make things by hand because they like to. And sometimes they make things so that they can sell them.

In markets and bazaars around the world, there are buyers for handmade goods. Why? Because they don't want look-alike things made in factories. They want one-of-a-kind things made by skilled craftsmen.

Afghanistan

Using hand tools, craftsmen in a shop in Herat make copper pots, pans, and jugs.

United States

A woman in Appalachia sews a patchwork quilt. The people of this eastern mountain region are known for their beautiful craftwork.

To market, to market

"Burro! Please move," begged Maria.

Burro, the family's stubborn donkey, did not want to carry Maria and her two large sacks to market. But a light touch of the whip did the trick. *Burro* began to clip-clop down the narrow, rocky road.

Maria and her family live in Guatemala, a country in Central America. Maria is on her way to the market place in Santiago Atitlán. *Burro* is carrying a large sack of maize (corn) and another sack of wheat. Maria hopes to sell the maize and wheat to shoppers on the market street in the town.

When they arrive in Santiago Atitlán, even *Burro's* ears perk up. Everyone is talking, laughing, and bargaining. As the donkey sways down the street, Maria looks about her. There are people selling fruits and vegetables. Others have handwoven baskets, rugs, and other articles for sale. Maria loves the sights and smells of the market place.

There are market places in almost every city in every country. If you are English, you might go to a greengrocer's for fruits and vegetables and to a fishmonger's for fish and fowl. In the United States, you might go to a large shopping center. Or in Mexico, Italy, and South Africa, you might travel to an outdoor market. There you would buy or sell goods, just as Maria does.

Guatemala

Indians buy, sell, or trade crops and other wares at this outdoor market in Santiago Atitlán.

Woodfield is a modern indoor
shopping center in Illinois.
It has many shops where gifts
and clothing are sold.

Philippines

A dugout canoe called a *banca* is used as a ferryboat. It takes passengers across a river in the Philippines.

May I help you?

"*¿En que puedo servirle?*" the guard asked.
"*May maitutulong ba ako?*" the boatman asked.
"*Darf Ich Ihnen helfen?*" the policeman asked.
"*Puis-je vous servir?*" the waiter asked.
"*Czy moge pani pomóc?*" the salesclerk asked.

What do all these people want to know? They are asking, "May I help you?" in Spanish, Pilipino, German, French, and Polish.

In Madrid, Spain, a guard at the Prado, the famous art museum, will tell you where you can see the paintings of the great artist El Greco. In the Philippines, the man who runs the ferryboat will take you across the river.

If you should get lost in Bonn, Germany, a policeman will help you to find your way. In Tunis, a city in Tunisia, a waiter will take your food order in Arabic or in French. In Warsaw, Poland, a salesclerk will help you to select a piece of fine porcelain for a present.

All of these people, and others like them, earn a living by helping people.

Tunisia

In the North African city of Tunis, a waiter makes an art of pouring a cup of coffee.

Bulgaria

At a gas station in Bulgaria, in southeastern Europe, an attendant helps a motorist.

France

French firemen, like firemen everywhere, fight fires to save lives and property.

Omar Alái's workday

"Insects, sheep, leaves, roots, and bark! That's what this rug is made of," says Omar as he sits at the loom. Omar remembers visiting the dye house. Here, he had watched the wool being dyed. And the dye was made from parts of plants and animals.

Omar Alái lives and works in the home of a master weaver. He is learning the craft. Instead of going to school, Omar weaves beautiful Persian rugs. The rugs are named for his town of Kerman, Iran. Kerman rugs are famous for their silklike wool and pale colors.

Today, Omar and five others are weaving a large carpet with a hunting scene. Omar is proud of this rug. After several thousand hours of work, it is almost finished. It will be a valuable rug.

Some children have to work to buy food and clothing for their families. Others work by helping out on the family farm or in the family store. And some don't have to work at all. But they often do. They want to have money of their own, to spend as they wish.

Iran

Many Iranian boys work as rug weavers. While they are learning the craft, they live and work in the home of a master weaver. He teaches them the skills they need to know.

Morocco

A Moroccan boy uses a camel and a donkey to plow the fields on his family's farm. Like all farm boys, he must do his share of the work.

United States

In the United States, girls and boys deliver newspapers to earn extra money.

An ancient theater at Epidaurus, Greece.

Time for Fun

What's the most fun for you? Do you like to shoot marbles? Do you like to swim, or ski, or go camping? Do you like to read, or draw, or make things?

People have always thought of ways to have fun. The ancient Greeks enjoyed running races and going to plays. The children of ancient Rome made their own toys and played blindman's buff. The people of Greece and China have been flying kites for more than 2,000 years. Fairs, plays, and puppet shows have been popular for hundreds of years.

Today, we still have fun doing all these things. But we have many other ways to have fun, too. We go surfing, skiing, and skin diving. We watch our favorite teams play games such as football and cricket. We go to zoos, museums, and parks.

The fact is, we like to have fun. We always have and we always will.

An African child playing with a toy truck.

Quick hands, quick eyes

Papua New Guinea

It's hard to make a good cat's cradle. But children all over the world enjoy this game.

Ten quick fingers can crisscross a string into a cat's cradle in seconds. It's almost like magic.

Most people play cat's cradle for fun. But some people believe that a cat's cradle has magic powers!

In Papua New Guinea, the people depend on a kind of potato called a yam for most of their food. At planting time, children and grown-ups make cat's cradles. When the yams begin to grow, the people use the string from the cat's cradles to tie the vines to sticks. They believe the string has a magic power to make the yams grow bigger and better.

In the United States, a game called jacks also takes quick hands and eyes. Jacks are small metal pieces. The jacks are placed on the floor. Then a player tries to pick up one or more of them while tossing and catching a ball.

This same game is played in India, where it is called *guttak*. But instead of jacks and a ball, players use small stones. Filipino children also play this game. They call it *sonca*.

Marbles is another quick-hand, quick-eye game that is played around the world. In the United States, children play a game of marbles called ringer. A player uses a big marble called a shooter to knock smaller marbles out of a ring.

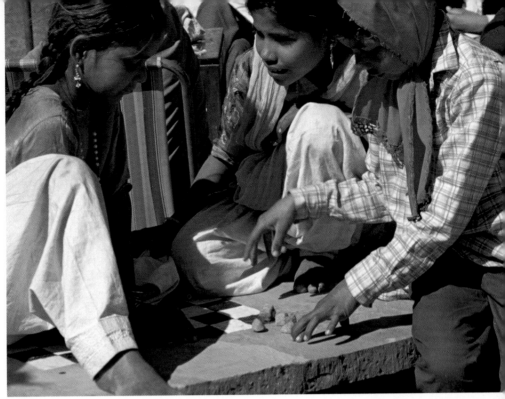

India

Girls use small stones to play a game
called *guttak.* It is much like the
game of jacks played in the United States.

In Alaska, Eskimo children play
a string game that calls for
quick hands and quick eyes.

United States

United States

A game of marbles is fun. The
one who shoots the most
marbles out of the ring, wins.

Taiwan

Chinese children play *tsoo, tsoo,* a "find me, catch me" game like blindman's buff.

Russia

Kindergarten children stay in their places while they act out a "find me, catch me" game. They are pretending to look for someone who is hiding.

Find me, catch me!

It's Alfredo's turn to be "blind hen." Pedro ties a big, red handkerchief over Alfredo's eyes. Then Pedro, Inez, Maria, and Juan form a circle around Alfredo. The four of them begin to chant, "Blind hen, blind hen, what have you lost?"

"I've lost a thimble and a needle," Alfredo replies.

"Where have you lost them?" ask the others.

"In a haystack," says Alfredo.

Inez steps into the circle. She turns Alfredo around three times and steps back. Now the children begin to tease Alfredo. They run up to him and shout, "Blind hen, blind hen."

Alfredo reaches out to catch them. But he is dizzy from being turned around. It is as black as night behind the blindfold. Besides, the children are careful to move away whenever Alfredo's hands come close to them. Then Juan gets careless. Alfredo grabs Juan's poncho. Now it is Juan's turn to be "blind hen."

Alfredo and his friends live in Peru. But "find me, catch me" games like blind hen are played in other parts of the world.

When Roman children played this game about 2,000 years ago, they called it *murinda*. Nowadays, Italian children know it as *mosca cieca*. Chinese children call it *tsoo, tsoo*. German children call it *blindekuh*. And in the United States, children call it blindman's buff.

What do you call it?

Three cheers for our side

People are crowding into the Olympic Stadium in Rome. Banners are flying. Flags are waving. Everyone is talking at once. *"Come sta?"* ("How are you?") *"Mi tanto piacere vederla!"* ("I'm so pleased to see you!")

The *calcio* champions from Rome and Milan are about to meet. *Calcio* is the Italian name for soccer. Every Sunday, from October to May, teams from the big Italian cities play one another.

"Evviva!" ("Hurrah!") A great roar echoes through the stadium as the game begins. Suddenly, the Milan fans start to whistle. They are angry. They think the referee has been unfair.

But the Rome fans hiss. They are happy with the referee's decision. There are always fans who are happy or unhappy with the referee!

Every country has one or more favorite sports. In Japan, men and women enjoy volleyball, a game that was invented in the United States. The Japanese have sent some fine volleyball teams to the Olympics. But soccer is probably the most popular sport in the world. It is the "national game" in many countries in Europe, South America, and Asia.

(continued on page 150)

Italy

Italian soccer fans get very excited about their "national sport." They wave banners and give deafening cheers when their favorite team scores.

Japan

Two members of a Japanese women's volleyball team leap high in the air to block a shot. This fast-moving game is played in more than 100 countries.

Mexico

The stands are filled for this soccer match between teams from Italy and Brazil.

Three cheers for our side

(continued from page 149)

Canada

Hockey is Canada's "national sport."
Invented on frozen Canadian lakes
and ponds, the game is now popular in
Western Europe, Russia, and Japan.

United States

Rodeos are popular in the United States and
Canada. This broncobuster hangs on in an
event at the Roundup in Pendleton, Oregon.

England

Cricket is England's favorite
summer sport. It is also a
popular game in Australia, the
West Indies, Pakistan, and
other places where the English
have introduced it.

Vacation time

A vacation is a time to forget work and worries. It's a time to have fun, or a time to rest. It's a time for families to do things together.

Some families like to take trips to faraway places. Other families may decide to explore nearby towns and villages. If people live in the city, they may enjoy going to the country. If they live on a farm, they may want to have fun in a big city.

Most families take vacations in the summer. But winter vacations are becoming very popular. Japanese families enjoy skiing. They may go to the mountains on the islands of Honshu or Hokkaido. There they race down the snow-covered slopes in the crisp, cold air.

France

Camping is a fun way for French families to spend a summer vacation.

Many French families enjoy summer camping trips. They pitch their tents in thousands of campsites operated by the government. These families have fun outdoors. They enjoy quiet, green forests and parks far from crowded, noisy city streets.

In the United States and Canada, some families take vacations at Christmastime, when schools are closed. If they want to get away from the cold, they may go to Florida. There they can skim over the surface of a lake on water skis. They can sail boats or go swimming. Or they can just lie in the hot sun.

No matter where in the world families live, they need a change from doing everyday things. That's what vacations are for. Where would you like to go on your next vacation?

Japan

Skiing is a favorite winter sport in the mountains of Japan.

United States

From Siberia to Greenland, Eskimo children care for and play with puppies that will grow up to become sled dogs.

Italy

A crowded, narrow street is a far cry from the open range. But riding a pony is a treat for this Italian boy.

How to bathe a buffalo

Water buffaloes love the water. That's why they are called water buffaloes. In Asia they are used to plow fields and rice paddies.

Water buffaloes are not pets. They are work animals. But children have fun with them anyway. Most of all, they enjoy giving the buffaloes a bath.

Water buffaloes hate the heat. They simply won't work when it is too hot. So, in the heat of the day the children ride water buffaloes to the nearest lake or river. There the buffaloes sink into the water. With only their eyes and noses showing, they wallow happily in the soft, cool mud.

Thai children have fun riding water buffaloes and giving them a bath in the river.

Thailand

In the meantime, the children swim and splash around them. This is the children's time to play. When the air has cooled, the children scrub the buffaloes until they are clean. Then they ride the buffaloes back to the fields and paddies to finish the day's work.

Eskimo dogs are work animals, too. The Eskimos use them to pull sleds. They also use them for hunting. Full-grown Eskimo dogs are not very friendly. But as puppies, they are cute. So Eskimo children play with the puppies and treat them like pets.

Children love animals. If they take care of their animals, children can learn a sense of responsibility. But most of all, animals are fun to play with. It does not matter if they are pets or work animals.

Carnivals, circuses, and puppet shows

A meadow is usually a place for sheep and cows. But not when a carnival or circus comes to town. Then it's a perfect place to pitch tents and put up rides.

In Munich, Germany, in the state of Bavaria, there's a place called Theresa Meadow. Every year, from the next to the last Sunday in September to the first Sunday in October, the *Oktoberfest,* or October feast, is held here. The *Oktoberfest* celebrates the wedding of a Bavarian king, held more than 150 years ago. The meadow is named in honor of his queen.

At the *Oktoberfest,* you'll ride on merry-go-rounds, swings, and Ferris wheels. You'll see people dressed in colorful costumes doing folk dances. And you'll feast on all kinds of goodies.

But perhaps you'd rather go to a circus in Romania. Here, you'll thrill to the tricks of performing elephants. You'll catch your breath as people swing from trapezes or walk a tightrope high above you. And you'll laugh at the silly things the clowns do.

Or what about seeing a puppet show? If you like to laugh, there's nothing funnier than *Punch and Judy,* a puppet play that's popular in England. But you can see puppet shows in almost any country. Sometimes you can see them at carnivals and circuses. And they are often held in theaters or in parks.

Do these carnivals and circuses and puppet shows seem like the ones you've been to? Of course they do. That's because they are much the same everywhere. They are fun places for children and grown-ups alike.

Romania

Three pretty girls thrill a circus audience in a daring act with huge elephants.

The *Oktoberfest,* or October feast, is a time for fun. Everyone enjoys the exciting rides.

West Germany

United States

Young children in Illinois are enchanted by this puppet show. Some countries in Europe have puppet heroes who speak and act like the people of the region.

Who's a toymaker?

All children are toymakers. Sticks and stones, boxes and bones—all sorts of throwaway things—can be made into toys. Toys are as much fun to make as they are to play with. All you need are some odds and ends and lots of imagination!

A big box is an ocean liner sailing over the sea. Or it can be a spaceship landing on the moon. It can even be a stagecoach rumbling through a mountain pass.

A worn old broom can be a camel racing across the sands of the Sahara. Bits of cloth and cardboard can be turned into puppets for a play. And with an old tire, some rope, and a tree, you can soon make a great swing.

Children make toys out of all sorts of things. In Bermuda, they make dolls from banana stalks and nuts. Swedish girls use rolled-up birchbark. In the United States and other places, children make funny little dolls out of corncobs. Mexican children turn cornhusks into toy donkeys. In the Solomon Islands, boys use large nuts to make twirling tops. And everywhere, boys and girls make kites to fly high in the sky on a bright, breezy day.

United States

Children enjoy a swing they made with an old tire and a strong piece of rope.

Indonesia

Dyak boys on the island of Borneo try their skills in a top contest.

South West Africa

A Hottentot boy plays with a toy truck he has put together from odds and ends.

Go fly a kite!

When someone says, "Go fly a kite!" they mean "Go away, get lost!" And that's just what happens to a kite when the string isn't strong enough. A hard wind blows and snaps the string. Your kite is lost. That's a sad moment. But when there's a good breeze—and you have a strong string—nothing is more fun than flying a kite.

Children around the world fly kites just for fun. But kites have other uses, too. They are used to send and receive radio signals. And water skiers use kites to pull themselves from the surface of the water into the air.

An old Korean story tells how, about a thousand years ago, a general won a battle with a kite. On a dark night, he tied a lantern to a kite. Then he flew the kite, with a lighted lantern, above the enemy camp. When the enemy soldiers saw the strange yellow light in the sky, they threw down their weapons. They thought the end of the world had come! The clever general attacked and defeated the enemy.

Nobody knows if this story is true. But we do know that when Korean children ask for toys, their mothers tie a list to the tail of a kite. The children fly the kites to tell the gods what they want. It's a custom—like sending a letter to Santa Claus.

Greece

Men and boys enjoy an afternoon of kite flying in Athens. The old, ruined buildings in the distance are on a famous hill called the Acropolis.

United States

The Sugar Plum Fairy, the Little Prince, and the Little Princess dance their parts in *The Nutcracker* ballet.

Canada

Actors give a performance of *Twelfth Night,* a play by William Shakespeare, at the Stratford Festival in Ontario.

Indonesia

On the island of Java, masked dancers act out an ancient Hindu story. The dancers imitate the stiff movements of puppets.

Curtain going up!

A sudden hush falls over the theater. As the lights dim, the curtain goes up. And there, on the brightly lighted stage, a story comes alive.

Most plays are stories in which the actors speak their parts. Operas are stories in which the performers sing their parts. And in ballet, the stories are acted out by dancing to special music.

All over the world, people enjoy going to the theater to see acted-out stories of real or make-believe happenings. Usually, the actors are people. Sometimes, the actors are puppets imitating people. But in Indonesia, human actors imitate puppets!

This kind of acting is called *wayang orang*, which means a play with "human puppets." *Wayang orang* actors often wear strange, scary masks and fanciful costumes. They act out ancient tales from the Hindu book *Ramayana*. The book tells of the adventures of a handsome young Hindu prince named Rama and his beautiful wife Sita.

The actors dance their parts to the music of the *gamelan* (orchestra). They move stiffly—like puppets. Why do they do this? Because for thousands of years the only actors in Indonesia were puppets. So when people decided to become actors, they simply imitated the puppets' movements.

People making the laws in England about 150 years ago.

Living Together

What is the first thing you must do before you can play a new game?

You must learn the rules. There have to be rules so the players will know what to do. If everyone played his own way, the game would be all mixed up.

Rules are a way to keep things from getting mixed up. We need rules for games. We also need rules to live by. Families have rules. Clubs have rules. Teams have rules.

Very strong rules are called laws. Laws are made by the leaders of a tribe or country. We have policemen, judges, and other people who see that laws are obeyed.

There are also rules that are not really rules. These are what we call polite customs or ways of behaving. Going to the end of a line, instead of cutting in, is a polite custom.

Everywhere in the world, people have rules, laws, and polite customs that work best for them. These rules, laws, and customs make it easier to work and play and live together.

People making the laws in West Germany today.

Do we have to?

"Aw, come on! Let's play one more game."

"We can't. We have to go home now."

David and Betty didn't want to leave. They were having too much fun. But helping to set the table is a rule in their family. It was getting close to suppertime. If they didn't hurry, they'd be late.

There are other rules in their family, too. There are rules for bedtime. There are health rules. And there are rules for doing things—like taking out the garbage and cleaning up their rooms.

Like most people, David and Betty sometimes try to get out of doing what they are supposed to do. Once in a while, David "forgets" to take out the garbage. And he often complains about having to wash his hands before he eats.

There are times when Betty leaves her room in a mess because she doesn't feel like putting away her toys. And she almost always fusses about having to go to bed before David, just because she is younger.

But most of the time, David and Betty are good about obeying the rules. They know that families everywhere have rules. It's the only way each person can know what is expected of him. And obeying the rules makes living together easier and more enjoyable for everyone.

United States

Taking out the garbage is a daily task for many children.

Peru

A young girl brings home a
bundle of firewood. This is
a task she must do every day.

Jordan

Among Arab people, it is a custom
for a son to be with his father
when coffee is served to a visitor.

Hong Kong

A boy takes his daily bath at the well,
while his sister polishes a pair of shoes.

We wait our turn

Tom was visiting his cousin Colin in London, England. It was Saturday. The boys were on their way to the Tower of London to see the royal jewels.

At the bus stop, Colin got in line behind the other people. Tom thought this rather strange. In New York City, he was used to people standing around any which way until the bus came. Then they would shove and push to get on.

"Is there a law here that says people must stand in line to wait for a bus?" Tom asked.

"Of course not," replied Colin. "But to tell the truth, I never thought about it before. We always stand in line. It's called 'queuing up.' It's a custom."

When people behave in a certain way for a long time, this way of doing things often becomes a custom. Customs are not the same everywhere. In some places a custom can be as important as a law. People may even be punished for disobeying a custom.

Queuing up is not an important custom. But English people do it because it makes life easier for everyone.

Spain

Bus riders in Madrid wait their turn. Some of them use the time to catch up on the news.

Children line up to use the slide in a city park. They know that this is the fair way to do it.

United States

Pulling together

A rowing team is a group of people working together. If each man pulled his oar when he felt like it, the team would never get anywhere—much less win a race.

So, like all teams, they have a leader. A rowing team leader is called a coxswain. He steers the boat. He also calls out the timing to the man who sits nearest to him. This man sets the pace for the other oarsmen. This way, they all pull together.

France

A rowing team must pull together to win. These eight-man French crews practice until they can row as one man. They pull their oars to the count of the coxswain, who sits facing them.

People must often work together to get a job done.
If it is a big job, they will meet to talk about how
to do it. Usually, they appoint or elect a leader.
Then they make a plan and discuss how to carry it out.
They make up rules and agree to follow them. The
leader directs the work of the group. He or she sees
to it that each person does his part.

This is the way a team plays a game. This is the way
people govern a town or a country. If we want to get
things done, we have to pull together.

United States

In 1968 and 1972, the people of the United States chose Richard Nixon to be their leader.

Ghana

A government official of Ghana welcomes the leader of Upper Volta—its president.

Yugoslavia

Queen Elizabeth of England visits the leader of Yugoslavia, President Tito.

Follow the leader

A school has a principal. A football team has a quarterback. An army has a general. All these people are leaders. It's their job to run the school, or the team, or the army.

Countries have leaders, too. And it's their job to run their country. But not all countries have the same kinds of leaders.

In many countries, people choose their leader by voting. The leader is usually called president, or prime minister, or premier. If the people don't like the way this person runs the country, they can vote for a new leader after a while. Some of the countries that choose their leaders are the United States, Great Britain, France, Canada, Mexico, and India.

In some countries, the leader is a king or queen. A king or queen isn't chosen by the people. He or she is usually a member of a family called the royal family. When the king or queen dies, another member of the royal family becomes king or queen. Some countries that have kings as leaders are Jordan, Saudi Arabia, Kuwait, and Swaziland. England and Holland have queens, and Sweden and Norway have kings. But they aren't really the leaders of these countries. Prime ministers, chosen by the people, are the real leaders.

Some countries have leaders that are chosen for life. When they die, a new leader is chosen. Yugoslavia is such a country, and its leader is called president. China is such a country, and its leader is called chairman. In Spain, the leader is called—the leader.

It's the law!

Each family has rules. Parents make them. Brothers and sisters sometimes get a chance to decide what the rules will be. Once the rules are made, the children are expected to obey them.

Of course, nobody is arrested for breaking a family rule. There are other punishments—doing extra work around the house, or not being able to go out and play, or even a spanking. Sometimes, if a child has a very good excuse, there may not be any punishment.

All families belong to one or more bigger "families." This may be a tribe, a town, a city, a state, a nation. Each of these has rules that are called laws. There is no excuse for breaking any of these laws. All law breakers are punished.

Who makes these laws?

A tribe has a chief and a council to make tribal laws. In some towns, the people meet to make the laws. All the grown-ups have a chance to take part.

Great numbers of people live in cities, states, and nations. There are too many people to meet together in one place to make the laws. So they elect a few people to meet and make the laws for them.

After the laws are passed, the police and the courts see to it that everyone obeys the laws.

West Germany

The Parliament Building in Bonn is called the *Bundeshaus.* Its members vote on laws.

Canada

A meeting to solve the city's problems
is held in Toronto's new City Hall.

United States

Town meetings are held in
New England. The citizens
discuss ideas and vote on them.

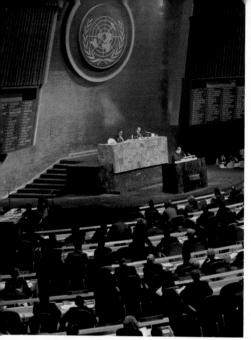

United Nations

People from 132 nations meet at the United Nations.

Athletes from 121 nations open the 1972 Summer Olympics in West Germany.

Olympic Games

The family of nations

The biggest "family" in the world is the United Nations. It has 132 members —almost every nation in the world.

Each nation sends people to represent it at United Nations headquarters in New York City. These people meet for about three months each year. They work together to keep peace in the world. They talk about how nations should behave toward one another. They talk about rules to protect the rights of everyone. They try to help people in many ways.

The Olympic Games is another world "family." Every four years, athletes from nations throughout the world compete in sports at the Olympic Games.

There are Boy Scouts in more than 100 nations. All Scouts have the same beliefs and purposes. They are taught to love God, their country, and other people. Every four years, Scouts from different countries meet at a world jamboree.

More than 80 countries belong to the World Association of Girl Guides and Girl Scouts. The girls, like the boys, learn ideals of character and love of country. Girls from around the world can meet at "world houses" in England, Mexico, Switzerland, and India.

In all these groups, people of different races, religions, and ways of life work and play together. They learn to know and respect one another in spite of their differences.

Boy Scouts

Scouts from many nations have a chance to meet every four years at a world jamboree.

An ancient Indian temple in Mexico.

We Believe

Most people in every age and in every place have believed in a power or powers greater than themselves. This belief in a greater power is called religion.

There are many different religions. Each has its own special beliefs and ways to worship. Even people of the same religion may practice their faith in many different ways.

Some religions believe in one God. Some believe in many gods. Some believe that there are spirits in animals, trees, and rocks. And some religions are a way of living rather than a way of believing.

In many parts of the world, people have built great temples and churches where they can worship. Other people have built large parks where they can go to worship nature gods. Others have no places of worship.

In this Section you will meet children of nine religious faiths. You will learn some of the things they are taught to believe, and some of the ways they worship. Some of their beliefs may seem strange. But your beliefs may seem just as strange to them.

A modern Buddhist temple in South Vietnam.

Manohar's religion

Brrr! Manohar shivers as his mother pours water over him. He is standing outside his house in the village of Amtala, India, and the morning air is cold on his bare skin. But he must bathe first thing each morning, right after he wakes up. This is a law of his religion.

When Manohar has bathed, he goes into the kitchen. Above the stove is a shelf on which stands a picture of the god Siva. Each morning Manohar puts a few grains of rice or a flower before the picture as an offering. He presses the palms of his hands together and bows his head. His mother lights a stick of sweet-smelling incense for the god. Then, with yellowish paste, Manohar puts a round mark on his forehead that shows he is a follower of Siva.

Manohar knows that while Siva is one of the greatest gods, there are many others. Ganesha, the god of luck, has a man's body and an elephant's head. The god Hanuman is a monkey. But Manohar knows that all the gods are just different shapes of Brahman, the one great power that rules all things.

Manohar believes that when he dies he will be born again, to start a new life in a new body. If he is good and kind to everyone while he is alive, he may be a rich man or a priest in his next life. But if he is bad, he may be a dog, a snake, or even an insect!

Manohar is a Hindu. Hinduism is one of the oldest of all religions, and the largest religion in India.

Hindus must bathe each day. This mother is bathing her children at a temple.

Nepal

Ceylon

In a Hindu home there is a shrine for the family's gods.

Deborah's religion

The afternoon sun is a big, red ball hanging low in the sky. Many of the people in the city of Tel Aviv-Yafo, in Israel, are hurrying home. It is Friday, and soon the sun will set. From then until the sun goes down on Saturday, it will be the Sabbath.

Deborah watches as her mother lights the Sabbath candles. The soft glow makes the room seem warm and cozy. Deborah's father blesses the family's wine and bread. Then they sit down to their Sabbath supper.

On Saturday, Deborah's father does not go to work.

The Sabbath is a time of rest, in honor of the day God rested after He finished making the world. In the morning, Deborah and her parents go to a temple, or synagogue, to worship.

In the synagogue, men read lessons from the Bible and say prayers. Many of the prayers are sung by a man called a cantor. A large scroll, called the Torah, is carried through the synagogue. The Laws of God are written on this scroll. At the front of the synagogue, seven candles flicker in a candleholder with seven branches. This is a Menorah, a symbol of Deborah's religion. The seven branches stand for the first seven days when God made everything.

Deborah believes in one God who made everything and who rules everything. She loves and respects God, tries to obey His laws, and to be good and kind. She believes that someday God will send a Messiah, a man who will end all of the world's troubles.

Deborah is a Jew. Her religion is called Judaism. It is the religion of the country of Israel, where she lives. It is also the religion of millions of Jewish people in all parts of the world.

Jews gather for worship in a synagogue.

United States

United States

The Jewish Sabbath starts at sunset on Friday. Here, the mother lights the Sabbath candles.

Rudi's religion

Ding! Dong! Come to church!

It's Sunday morning in the town of Landeck,
Austria. The big bell in the steeple of Rudi's church
is ringing to remind people to come and worship God.

The inside of Rudi's church is very beautiful. There
are colored pictures painted on some of the walls.
There are statues of Jesus Christ, of Christ's mother,
Mary, and of many saints. Candles glow and flicker
everywhere. The sun shining through the stained-glass
windows makes them look like bright paintings.

The priest leads the people in prayers and songs. He reads a lesson from the Bible and gives a sermon. He blesses a cup of wine and thin, round pieces of bread called Hosts. Then Rudi and others go up to the altar and kneel. The priest puts a Host into each one's mouth. Now they have shared a sacred meal as God's family.

Rudi believes that about 2,000 years ago, God sent His son to earth as a man called Jesus Christ. Christ taught people to live good, kind lives. His enemies killed Him by nailing Him to a cross. But Rudi believes that Christ came back to life and went up to heaven. Rudi believes that if he follows Christ's teachings he will go to heaven, too. All people who follow Christ's teachings are called Christians.

Rudi is a Roman Catholic. The largest of all Christian groups, the Roman Catholic Church has followers in every part of the world.

The pope is the head of the Roman Catholic Church.

Vatican City

United States

Some Roman Catholic churches have services in which young people play guitars and sing.

Chitra's religion

What will I be when I am born again? wonders
Chitra. I'd hate to be a pig, but I suppose that's what
I'll be if I'm bad!

But I won't be bad, she tells herself. I'll do all the
things the Buddha said to do. I'll be kind to
everyone. I'll give everything I have to poor people.
Maybe, if I'm *very* good, I won't have to be born
again at all. Maybe I will achieve nirvana when I die.
Then I will be in perfect peace forever!

Chitra is in a temple in the city of Colombo,

Ceylon. She kneels before a big golden statue of the Buddha. Chitra and others come to the temple to sit and think hard, for a long time, about the things that the Buddha taught.

There is also a little statue of the Buddha in Chitra's house. Each evening, her family sits before it for a while to think about the Buddha's teachings.

Chitra knows that the Buddha was a rich prince who lived in India long ago. This prince gave away all his riches and became a wanderer. One day, as he sat under a banyan tree, the truth about all things came into his mind and he became the Buddha.

The word "buddha" means "to be wise." The Buddha taught his followers that only if they stop wanting things can they achieve nirvana when they die. They must also be helpful and kind to all people, especially their enemies.

Chitra is a Buddhist. Buddhism began in northern India, but has since spread to Tibet, China, Japan, and most of Southeast Asia.

Ceylon

Buddhist shrines in Ceylon are called dagobas.

South Vietnam

Big statues of the Buddha are in many Buddhist temples.

Hammet's religion

It is early morning in the city of Oran, in Algeria.
The sun is not up yet, and most people are asleep.
But from tall towers, called minarets, come the voices
of men known as "callers." They shout out a kind
of song:

> "God is great!
> I say there is no god but the One God.
> I say that Mohammed is the messenger of God.
> Come to prayer. Prayer is better than sleep."

Soon, Hammet and his father are hurrying to pray

at their place of worship, a building called a mosque. Hammet's mother stays at home to pray.

Hammet and his father carry little rugs called prayer mats. After washing themselves at a fountain, they put their mats down on the mosque floor. They pray by kneeling on their mats and bending over to touch their foreheads to the floor. They pray this way five times a day, no matter where they are—at home, in the street, even out in the desert. When they pray they always face toward the holy city of Mecca, in Arabia.

Hammet believes that there is one great God who made all things. He believes that about 1,300 years ago God showed a man named Mohammed the way He wanted people to live and worship. Mohammed said that God wanted people to be good, to help others, and to honor and obey God. God's words were written in a book called the Koran.

Hammet is a Moslem. He belongs to the religion of Islam. "Islam" means "Obeying God." Hammet knows that if he does the things God wants, he will go to heaven when he dies.

Turkey

A Moslem house of worship is called a mosque.

Afghanistan

Moslems pray five times each day. They kneel on small rugs and face toward the holy city of Mecca in Saudi Arabia.

Sue's religion

Late again! Sue dashes up the steps of the small, white church in Atlanta, Georgia, and tugs open the door. Slipping inside, she hurries to her Sunday school class.

The Sunday school room is just a plain room with some tables and chairs in it. The children in the class sit at two long tables. As Sue enters, Mr. Martin, the Sunday school teacher, is reading from the Bible. The Bible is a very important part of Sue's religion. She believes it tells her how God wants her to live and behave. Sue believes that God made the world and everything in it. He sent His son, Jesus Christ, to earth to teach all people to be good and to save them from sin.

When Sue is older she will be baptized. She believes that before a person can be baptized he must be old enough to understand what baptism means. When she is baptized, her whole body will be dipped under water.

After Sunday school, the children go to the part of the church where services are held. They join the grown-ups in a big, plain room filled with benches. The service begins with everyone singing hymns. The minister reads from the Bible and gives a sermon.

Sue is a Baptist. Baptists are Christians and believe in the teachings of Jesus Christ. Baptists are also Protestants. Protestant is the name given to all Christian groups outside the Roman Catholic and Eastern Orthodox Churches. There are hundreds of Protestant groups, but the Baptist, Episcopalian, Lutheran, Methodist, and Presbyterian groups are among the largest.

United States

A Baptist Sunday school class has a Bible lesson. Many Protestant children go to Sunday school to study the Bible and learn the teachings of Christ.

Nikos' religion

Bong-bong! The happy sound of the bell, ringing
from the church that overlooks the little Greek town
of Pigadi, is telling Nikos to hurry. He runs the
last few steps to the church and goes to stand with the
men and boys. The girls and women stand together
on the other side of the aisle.

He is just in time. The priest, Father Sioris, walks
toward the altar. His helper swings the incense holder
so that its little bells tinkle. The incense fills the
church with a sweet, spicy smell.

Father Sioris goes through one of the doorways in
the partition that separates the altar from the rest
of the church. The partition is covered with icons—
pictures of Jesus Christ and of other holy people. Nikos
has found that no matter where he stands, the eyes in
the pictures always seem to be looking at him.

The service is long and musical. All the prayers,
lessons, and psalms are chanted or sung. When it
ends, Nikos hurries to the front of the church to get a
piece of the bread that Father Sioris has blessed.

Nikos is a Greek Orthodox Christian. He believes
that Jesus Christ, the Son of God, was sent from
heaven to save all people and to teach them how God
the Father loves them and wants them to live.

The Greek Orthodox Church is one of the Eastern
Churches. Eastern Orthodoxy is the largest and most
important Christian faith in Greece, Russia, and
other parts of eastern Europe and western Asia. It is
also one of the largest faiths in the United States.

Greece

These two priests are
conducting a Greek
Orthodox service. The
church is filled with
paintings called icons.

Fujiko's religion

Fujiko's feet go crunch-crunch as she walks along
the gravel path with her mother. The path winds
through a grove filled with trees, rocks, and ponds.
It is like a big park, but it is really a place of worship.
Many of the people from the town in Japan where
Fujiko lives come to this grove to pray. To enter
the grove, people go between two tall, upright posts
that have two other posts across the top. This is a
kind of gate, called a torii.

Fujiko looks at the trees and rocks as she walks

along. She knows there are gods and spirits in many of them. There are gods and spirits in almost everything —trees, rocks, mountains, fields, streams, rain, wind, fire, rice, corn, and other things. Many ancestors are also gods.

At the end of the long gravel path is a small wooden building. This is a holy place, called a shrine. Fujiko and her mother stand before it. They clap their hands and bow their heads in prayer.

Fujiko sees small shrines of this sort almost everywhere she goes. They are beside roads, in fields, and in towns, as well as in parklike groves. In Fujiko's home there is also a shrine, one that looks like a tiny cupboard. Each day Fujiko's father puts a jar of water and a vase filled with flowers or green leaves in front of the shrine to honor the family god.

Fujiko is a Shintoist. Shinto is the native religion of Japan. The word "Shinto" means "the Way of the Gods."

Japan

Fortunes, printed on pieces of paper, are hung from a tree at a Shinto shrine.

People wash their hands before praying at a Shinto shrine.

Japan

Ketwago's religion

It is almost night on the Kalahari Desert in southern Africa. As the sun sets, the sky turns red, then purple, then black. Ketwago watches the stars come out. He believes they are the eyes of people who have died.

Ketwago's father, Tose, has made the evening fire. Fire is a man-thing, so women may not start it, just as they may not hunt animals or touch bows and arrows. Only the men, and boys Ketwago's age and older, do the hunting. The women and girls search for melons, seeds, and roots to eat.

When food is scarce, everyone works hard. But at
night, everyone relaxes. All the men, women, and
children sit around the fire, enjoying its warmth
and eating. It is a time for storytelling, joking, and
dancing. Ketwago believes that the most important of
all things is to enjoy the company of other people.
He tries hard never to be quarrelsome, mean, or angry.
Sharing what he has with others is as natural to him
as breathing.

Ketwago believes that the world and all things in it
were made by Ntadima, who is everywhere and is
all-powerful. Ketwago does not pray to Ntadima, for
Ntadima is too great for that. But Ketwago tries not
to be proud or mean, for Ntadima does not like that.
And Ketwago believes that if a man kills more animals
than he needs for food, Ntadima will be angry.

Ketwago is one of a group of people called Bushmen.
The beliefs of the Bushmen have to do with their
practical, everyday needs. They are interested most
in finding food and living together happily.

Botswana

Bushmen do not have
priests or special places of
worship. Their religion is
simply their way of life.
They believe that one of
the most important parts
of life is being with friends
around the campfire.

This piece of stone, known as the Rosetta Stone, has writing carved in three languages. With it, wise men were able to unlock the secret of the long-forgotten picture language of ancient Egypt.

Show and Tell

What was the most important thing ever invented?
It was—language! With language, people can explain
ideas and trade thoughts. No animal can do that!
Communication—being able to share information—is
what made civilization possible.

Long after people learned to speak, they began to
write. They had no alphabet, so they drew pictures
that stood for ideas and words. The early Egyptians
had hundreds of signs for words or parts of words.

Like other ancient people, the Egyptians often wrote
on clay tablets or stones. It was from one such stone,
the Rosetta Stone, that we learned their language.

Later inventions gave us new ways to communicate.
The printing press gave us books. With the telegraph,
we could send messages over long distances. Then came
the telephone, phonograph, radio, motion pictures,
and television. Now we can talk to someone who is far
away. We can watch pictures of men walking on the
moon. But sitting down and talking with a friend is
still the best kind of communication.

Talking things over, as these two
Dutch children are doing, is still
the best kind of communication.

Japan

In Japan, people bow to each other when they meet.

Tibetans stick out their tongues as a sign of respect.

Tibet

Actions speak louder than words

When a person in Tibet wants to say to someone, "I respect you," he sticks his tongue out!

When two people meet in Japan, they bow.

And when a man in Yugoslavia wants to say, "Hi, pal," to a friend, he pinches his friend's cheek.

In Nigeria, people clap their hands when they meet someone they respect. It means, "I am honored." They also clap their hands when someone does them a favor. It's their way of saying, "Thanks."

All over the world, people have ways of saying things without words. After seeing a play, people in England and Russia clap their hands. They are saying to the

Yugoslavia

A pinch on the cheek is a friendly greeting and a sign of affection.

Nigeria

A mountain tribesman claps his hands to show respect and to say, "Thank you."

actors, "Thank you. We liked your performance." In England, the actors bow to the audience to say, "Thank you." But Russian actors clap. That's their way of saying, "Thank you for liking us."

When an American holds his hand away from him and moves his fingers up and down, he is saying "Good-by." When an Italian or a Peruvian does the same thing, he is saying, "Come here."

Sometimes a sound can mean something. When Americans click their tongues, they mean "too bad." And in the United States, "shhh" means "be quiet." But in Germany, "shhh" means "hurry up!"

We all make different sounds

When a dog barks, we all hear the same sound. But a French boy says that his dog is saying *"gnaf-gnaf!"* A German girl says her dog is saying *"wau-wau!"* And Japanese children say that their dogs are saying *"wung-wung!"* What does your dog say?

If all these children *hear* the same sound, why do they *say* the sound in different ways? It's because they speak different languages. All languages are made up of words. And words are sounds that stand for things. But every language has different sounds.

Suppose you want to tell your best friend that you have a dog. How would you say the word "dog"? If you speak Spanish, you'd say "pay roh" (*perro*). If you speak German, you'd say "hoont" (*hund*). And if you speak French, you'd say "shean" (*chien*). But if you and your friend don't speak the same language, he or she won't know what you are saying.

Sometimes, even people who speak the same language don't say words the same way. In the United States, people in Boston speak with a New England accent. They say "dahg." People in Atlanta speak with a Southern accent. They say "dawg." Both are saying the word "dog," but in a different way.

This is true in other countries, too. People from different parts of England often find it hard to understand one another. This sometimes happens at the Speaker's Corner, in Hyde Park, London. Here, anyone can make a speech about anything. But if the speaker comes from Yorkshire, in northern England, he may have a Yorkshire accent. If so, many Londoners may not understand him. There's no point in talking if people don't understand what you say.

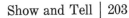

In Hyde Park, in London, there is a spot known as Speaker's Corner. Anyone who wants to can make a speech—about anything.

England

The Netherlands

There's nothing better than to have a friend to talk to. These two Dutch children are sharing thoughts about something they have found.

Denmark

Watch out! Your car will end up in the water if you don't stop when you see this warning sign.

Guatemala

A giant paintbrush shows everyone what can be bought in this store.

No words, just pictures!

In Afghanistan, there are roads for cars and trucks and roads for camels and donkeys. Even if a driver is from another country, he can tell which road is which by the picture signs.

Picture signs make it possible for almost anyone to understand basic information. A sign showing a car going into a canal quickly warns any driver of danger. If the sign had words, the driver would have to be able to read the language.

Picture signs are used throughout the world. You don't have to know even one of the world's 3,000 languages to understand a picture.

A picture sign shows truck drivers and camel drivers which road to take.

Afghanistan

Put it in writing

When you do your homework or write a letter to a friend, the marks you make on the paper stand for the sounds you make when you talk. Writing is a way of turning sounds into marks that fit together and make words.

No one knows who invented writing. But it's certainly a marvelous invention! With writing you can "talk" to someone who lives miles and miles away. With writing, people who own stores can make signs that tell what they sell. Whether you live in Cairo, Egypt, or Calais, France, you can find a movie theater or a butcher shop by looking for a sign.

Just as there are different languages all over the world, there are different kinds of writing. Arabic writing looks like flowing curves, with dots and dashes mixed in. Chinese writing looks like little squares, windows, and stick-figures.

But whatever kind of writing it may be, the marks stand for the sounds that the people make when they speak their language.

France

Models of a cow, lamb, and pig help you to know that the sign *"boucherie"* means "butcher shop" in the French language.

Egypt

Want to see a mystery movie? This Arabic sign tells about one that's showing in Cairo.

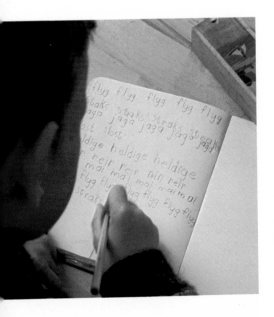

Norway

The marks this boy makes as he writes stand for the sounds he makes when he speaks Norwegian.

What's new?

Have the astronauts landed on the moon yet? Did our team win yesterday? Will it rain tomorrow?

Everyone wants to know what's happening. We're curious about things that go on everywhere. Thanks to the invention of printing, people all over the world can get the news in their newspapers.

Millions of newspapers are printed every day throughout the world. Nearly every country has at least one newspaper that comes out every day. Many big countries have hundreds of different newspapers. Some newspapers are made up of many pages and are

China

People stop on a street in Canton to get the latest news from "wall newspapers." New papers are pasted over the old ones. Sometimes there are 20 or 30 papers pasted one on top of the other.

printed on a huge printing press. Others may have only a single page that is printed on a small copying machine. Some are even written by hand.

In most countries, people buy their newspapers and bring them home to read. But in some places, newspapers are put up on the walls of buildings. It's a common sight in China to see crowds of people reading "wall newspapers."

In some parts of the world there are a great many people who are too poor to buy newspapers. To find out what's new, they read the wall newspapers. There are also many people who cannot read. So they go to listen while someone reads the news aloud.

Drum talk

"Listen!"

The two men stopped, every sense alert to the world around them. The air was filled with sound—birds screeching, monkeys chattering. But that was as it should be. The jungle is always full of noise. There were no strange sounds.

Then they heard it. The high and low notes of a drum. The sound could be heard clearly above the din of the jungle. They listened carefully as the drumbeats

A Wagenia tribesman beats out a message on a wooden drum.

Zaire

continued. Then, as suddenly as it had started, the drum stopped.

One man turned to the other. "Come," he said, "we are needed at the village."

How did they know they were needed? They had heard the message on the "jungle telegraph." In Zaire, Congo, and other countries in Africa, drums—or gongs, as they are called in Congo—are still used to send messages.

A gong is a big, hollow log with a long slot in it. Beaten on one side of the slot, it makes a low note. Beaten on the other side, it makes a high note. These two notes are like the high and low tones of the language.

To make a message clear, many words are often needed. It may take as many as 14 drumbeats to send one short word such as "dog." All messages are sent twice.

Every village has a gong. And every gong has a name. The name is beaten out at the beginning or end of the message. The gong at Yatuka village, in Congo, is called "Masters of the river." A nearby gong is named "The evil spirit has no friend or kin." The people of Yangomu village named their gong "Birds do not steal from a person without food."

A gong can be heard 2 to 10 miles away. But if you want to talk to someone on the other side of the world, you'll have to use a telephone.

Australia

A telephone "box" on a beach in Sydney doesn't look like a telephone "booth" in Moscow. But these young people could be talking to one another.

Russia

American Samoa

This worker in a television control room dresses in a comfortable, wrap-around skirt called a lava-lava.

American Samoa

These Polynesians sit on grass mats to watch television. The large poles hold up the thatched roof. Because the climate is warm, the house has open sides.

A window on the world

Long ago, people didn't get much news. They never even knew what happened a few miles away—unless someone who had been there told them. That was the only way to get news—someone had to tell you. And, usually, when you got the news it was very old.

Today, millions of people watch news as it happens —on television. People everywhere in the world watch television for news and for fun. But in many places schools also use television—to teach.

On the islands of American Samoa, in the South Pacific, TV is a very real part of education. Schools in Samoa are often grass huts. But there is a TV set in every school. The children are taught many of their subjects over TV. In fact, the TV system on the islands was set up for the children!

At night, though, there are news programs for the grown-ups. Then, Samoan families, like millions of other families, sit around to watch TV. They may live in grass huts on an island in the middle of the Pacific Ocean, but they know what is happening in the world.

Television is the newest way of spreading news and teaching things—of communicating. It's like a window that looks out upon the whole world. And it's helping to change the world.

Pen pals

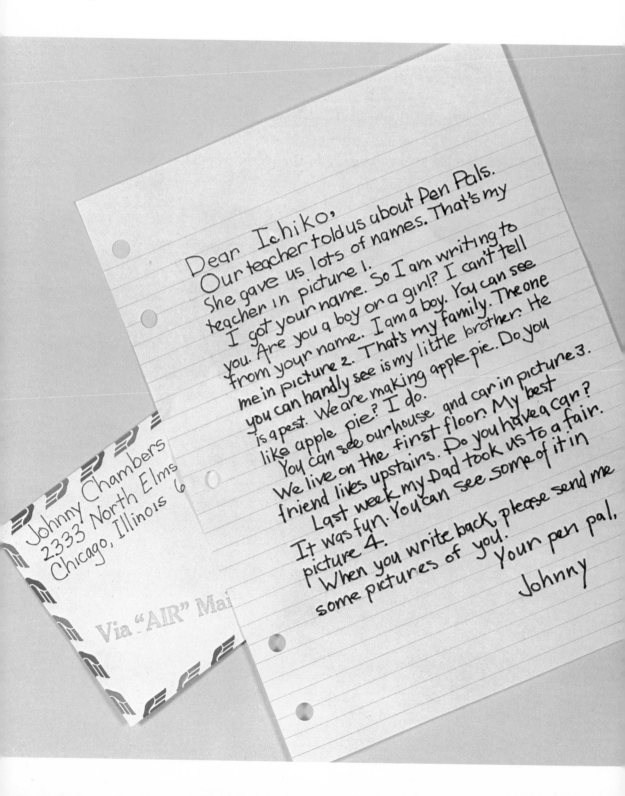

Dear Ichiko,

Our teacher told us about Pen Pals. She gave us lots of names. That's my teacher in picture 1. I got your name. So I am writing to you. Are you a boy or a girl? I can't tell from your name. I am a boy. You can see me in picture 2. That's my family. The one you can hardly see is my little brother. He is a pest. We are making apple pie. Do you like apple pie? I do.

You can see our house and car in picture 3. We live on the first floor. My best friend lives upstairs. Do you have a car? Last week my Dad took us to a fair. It was fun. You can see some of it in picture 4.

When you write back, please send me some pictures of you!

Your pen pal,

Johnny

Johnny Chambers
2333 North Elms
Chicago, Illinois 6

Via "AIR" Mai

(continued on page 216)

Pen pals
(continued from page 215)

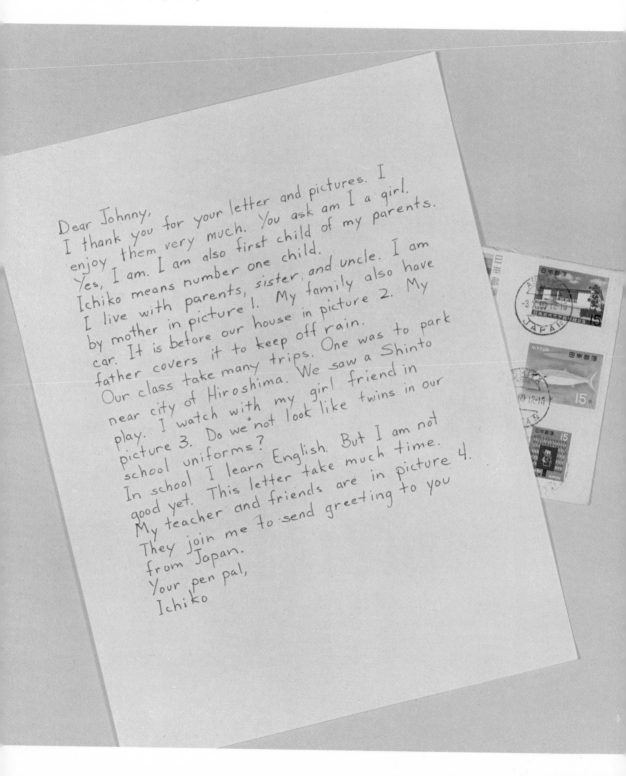

Dear Johnny,

I thank you for your letter and pictures. I enjoy them very much. You ask am I a girl. Yes, I am. I am also first child of my parents. Ichiko means number one child.

I live with parents, sister, and uncle. I am by mother in picture 1. My family also have car. It is before our house in picture 2. My father covers it to keep off rain.

Our class take many trips. One was to park near city of Hiroshima. We saw a Shinto play. I watch with my girl friend in picture 3. Do we not look like twins in our school uniforms?

In school I learn English. But I am not good yet. This letter take much time. My teacher and friends are in picture 4. They join me to send greeting to you from Japan.

Your pen pal,
Ichiko

The oldest wooden schoolhouse in the
United States, at St. Augustine, Florida.

How Do You Know?

Ketwago was learning to hunt. Pulling his bowstring tighter, he moved slowly forward.

"Stoop as low as you can," said his father from behind him. "When we stoop over, the antelopes think we are animals and do not run from us. Then you can get close enough to shoot your arrow."

Thousands of miles away, Karen was learning about health. "These are the foods you should have every day in order to stay healthy," said the teacher, pointing to pictures on a big chart.

Children around the world learn different things in different ways. Karen goes to school in a building and learns from teachers. Ketwago doesn't go to school at all. He learns from his father, and from the other grown-ups of his tribe.

Children learn from parents, from friends, from teachers. They learn in schools and out of them. Children everywhere need to know the things that will help them to live in their kind of world.

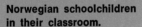

Norwegian schoolchildren in their classroom.

First lessons

Ketwago and his family live in the Kalahari Desert
in southern Africa. They belong to a group of people
known as Bushmen. Bushmen do not raise animals or
plants for food. Instead, the men and older boys hunt.
And the women and girls look for plants and roots.

When Ketwago was very young he made believe he
was a hunter, like his father. He pretended to stalk
caterpillars and beetles as they crawled and scuttled
across the dry earth. He waited and longed for the
time when his father would teach him to hunt.

One day, Ketwago's father took his son far from the

Botswana

A Bushman teaches his son to recognize the tracks of different animals. Bushmen hunt with poisoned arrows. They must be able to follow wounded animals for long distances.

camp. Slowly and patiently, he showed him how to recognize the tracks of certain animals. In the days to come, Ketwago would learn how to make a strong bow and how to shoot poisoned arrows with skill.

In the meantime, Ketwago's sister was learning from her mother. She was taught which plants and roots are safe to eat and where to find them. She also learned how to build a grass shelter called a skerm.

Among the Bushmen, children must learn to hunt, to find roots, and to build skerms. Without these skills, they might die. Ketwago and his sister do not go to a school. They learn from their parents and the people with whom they live.

Lebanon

What would it be like to go to school in another land? The children would look different. Their clothes would look different. The classroom and schoolyard would look different. And the language would be different. And yet, somehow, everything else would be much the same.

Peru

Thailand

Norway

Where do you go to school?

Thanon felt as if there were a thousand butterflies in his stomach. This would be his first day of school. He was now 8 years old, and in Thailand, where Thanon lives, this is when children start school.

Thanon didn't feel like eating breakfast. But, to please his mother, he did swallow a few mouthfuls of rice. Then he picked up his shoes and climbed down the ladder that led from the bamboo hut to the ground. He was careful not to dirty his new school uniform. When he reached the ground, he put on his shoes and started down the dirt road to school.

The school was the biggest and most beautiful building in the village. And no wonder, for it was also the village temple. Someday, the villagers hoped to have enough money for a school. But until then they would have to use the temple.

When Thanon arrived, the teacher was standing near the door. As he approached her, Thanon put the palms of his hands together just below his chin. Then he bowed his head slightly. This is how Thai children greet grown-ups and show respect for them. The teacher's warm smile made Thanon feel better.

In the classroom, the boys sat on one side and the girls on the other side. Thanon found a seat and sat down. Looking around, he saw that some of the others seemed a little frightened, too. He was glad to know that he was not the only one who felt this way.

A school is a place where people meet to learn from a teacher. It can be in a temple, a one-room schoolhouse, or any other kind of building. In fact, it doesn't even have to be in a building.

(continued on page 224)

Where do you go to school?
(continued from page 223)

Many small villages in Pakistan have no schoolhouses. Instead, classes are held outdoors. The children sit on the ground and write their lessons on small writing boards called slates. If they do not have slates, they write in the dirt with a stick.

In Australia, there are children who go to school at home. These children live far from cities and towns, in a lonely place Australians call the outback. Families here may live hundreds of miles apart. So the children listen and talk to a teacher over a two-way radio. If a family doesn't have a two-way radio, the children get their lessons in the mail.

In The Netherlands, France, and Germany, many children live on barges with their families. The barges travel up and down rivers and canals, carrying products from one town to another.

Classes are held outdoors in many villages in Pakistan.

Pakistan

France

Barge children study as they travel.
At cities along the way, they turn
in homework and get assignments.

In The Netherlands, barge children go to special
schools in the towns where the barges stop. While the
barges are tied up, the children attend classes. They
are also given lessons to do as they travel. In this
way, they can keep up with their schoolwork.

When the barge gets to the next stop, the children
go to another school. They turn in their homework, go
to classes, and get more homework to do.

When Dutch barge children complete the sixth
grade, they may be sent to live with a family on shore.
Then they can go to a regular school.

Special problems—special classes

Akibo kneels on the sloping roof. Putting down his bundle of thatch, he makes sure it is in exactly the right place. Then he ties it down so that it will not slip off.

The hot sun burns the back of his neck. The damp, rough straw scratches his bare legs. But Akibo hardly notices. He is too busy proving that he is the best student in his class.

On a roof top? Yes. Akibo is doing his school lessons. He and his classmates are learning how to build a house. The boys learn how to make the thatched roofs. The girls learn how to prepare the mixture of clay and water that they will plaster over branches to make the walls.

Akibo lives in a village in Malawi, a small country in southern Africa. All the houses in Akibo's village have mud walls and thatched roofs. Akibo and his people have always lived in such houses.

Akibo and the other children go to school to learn how to read, write, and do arithmetic. They learn many of the things that are taught in most schools. But they also learn things that are especially important for their way of life. One of the special things children in Malawi learn is how to build and repair their houses.

We all learn certain skills from our parents. We also learn other skills from our teachers in school. We may go to a class in hut making. Or, we may go to a class in driver education. The skills we learn are different because our ways of life are different. We learn the skills we need to know—the skills that are important for our way of life.

Malawi

Boys and girls in a hut-making class learn
how to build and repair the mud and grass huts
they live in. The boys work on the roof and
the girls mix the mud for the walls.

Colombia

These children go to school in dugout canoes. Their schoolhouse is built on stilts, like all the other houses.

Children in many countries walk to school, even on the coldest winter days.

Russia

Denmark

Many Danish students ride their bicycles to school.

How do you get to school?

Many children walk to school. Others ride their bikes. Some go to school in a car or a bus. But how do children get to school when they live in the middle of a lake?

In Colombia, South America, many families live in areas called *ciénagas*. A *ciénaga* is a big, shallow lake or a reed-filled marsh. Each house in a *ciénaga* village stands on stilts—even the schoolhouse. How do the children get to school? They climb into dugout canoes and paddle over. And because the weather is always warm, they can paddle to school all year round.

Children in Canada have a different problem. Here, the winters are long and cold. Deep snow covers the ground for months. So, many of the children have found a new way to get to school. They ride on snowmobiles!

What's a snowmobile? It's a kind of sled on skis. But it has a motor. Some snowmobiles are big enough to carry four persons. The driver uses handlebars to steer the snowmobile over ice and snow. It's an easy, fun way to get to school. How do you get to school?

Snowmobiles add excitement and fun to a trip to school.

Canada

In China there are many old stories about dragons.

Our Stories, Songs, and Sayings

Everywhere in the world, grown-ups have always told stories to children. Stories about dragons, giants, and fairies. Stories about warriors and great battles. Stories about animals that talk and act just like people.

Grown-ups also sing songs to children. They teach them dances. They teach them riddles and wise sayings that will help them when they grow up. Sometimes they talk to children about ghosts, evil spirits, and magical spells that will bring good luck and keep bad luck away. They tell them all the things their parents and grandparents told them.

As children grow older, they read myths, fairy tales, and fables in books. They learn other songs and sayings from teachers and friends. And when they have children of their own, they will become the storytellers. In this way, these stories, songs, and sayings are passed along from one generation to the next.

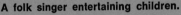
A folk singer entertaining children.

Tales of mighty warriors

Scaly dragons and knights in armor . . . magic swords and magic spells . . . great battles and deeds of courage! Nearly every part of the world has stories filled with such things—tales of mighty warriors who lived long ago and had wonderful adventures.

From England comes the story of King Arthur and his magic sword, Excalibur. Arthur and his Knights of the Round Table fought against evil and wickedness.

In Germany, Norway, Sweden, and Denmark, stories tell of a hero named Siegfried, or Sigurd. He killed the terrible dragon Fafnir. Then he freed the maiden Brunhilde from the ring of magic fire.

The people of Iran have the story of Rustem, who spent his life fighting his country's enemies. From Spain comes the hero called El Cid. He helped to drive invaders from Africa out of Spain. And France has the story of Roland and the knights of King Charlemagne.

For hundreds of years minstrels and storytellers sang and told stories about heroes in palaces and market places. Today, we hear these tales from the storyteller at the library, or read them in books. Through them, we share the adventures, joys, and sorrows of the hero. And we also discover the importance of courage, honor, and duty.

England

This scene from the story of King Arthur was painted by the American artist N. C. Wyeth. Many countries have such legends.

Animal tales

"You're a slowpoke!" said the Hare to the Tortoise. "If we were to have a race, I'd beat you by miles!"

"Let's have a race and see," suggested the Tortoise.

Off they went. The Hare was soon far ahead. When he looked back, he couldn't even see the Tortoise. "He'll never catch up to me," thought the Hare. "I think I'll rest awhile." He lay down and fell fast asleep.

But the Tortoise kept plodding along. Before long he passed the sleeping Hare.

When the Hare awoke, he hurried to the finish line. And there, to his surprise, was the Tortoise, waiting for him. The Tortoise had won the race!

This story was first told in Greece, more than 2,500 years ago. It is one of Aesop's *Fables*. These *Fables* are stories in which animals talk and act like people. They do things that can teach people lessons. The lesson of the story of the Tortoise and the Hare is that it doesn't matter how fast you are—what is important is that you stick to the job.

Animal stories that teach lessons are told everywhere in the world. Most of them are thousands of years old.

In Africa, the Ashanti people of Ghana have stories about Anansi the Spider. He is always playing tricks on the other animals. His tricks usually get him into trouble.

Coyote is the hero of many American Indian animal tales. He is a trickster, too. And in Indonesia, people tell stories of Cousin Mouse-Deer, a little animal who uses tricks to protect himself.

Greece

Aesop was a Greek slave who told fables with
animal characters. These are some of the animals,
as painted by the English artist, Arthur Rackham.

Let's all sing

Do you know "Old MacDonald Had a Farm"? Or "The Frog Went A'Courting"? Or "Yankee Doodle"?

These are folk songs. Folk songs are songs that are made up by common people.

Many folk songs tell about heroes, bold robbers, or young sweethearts. Others, like "Old MacDonald," are just for fun. Some folk songs are about the kinds of work that people do. Christmas carols are folk songs, and so are spirituals, and many church hymns. And so are the patriotic songs of many countries.

Every country has its own folk songs. Most of these songs were made up long ago, and people have been singing them for hundreds of years.

One of the oldest American folk songs is "Turkey in the Straw." It's about silly things that happen to a young farmer. An old, old German song, "Nur Du," is about a young man who must leave his sweetheart. "Meadowlands" is an old Russian favorite that tells of the horsemen who roam the vast, rolling plains of Russia. The Canadian song "Alouette" is a fun song about a bird.

The songs that European minstrels sang at castle feasts and village fairs were folk songs. So are the songs of American cowboys, and of shepherds,

United States

These children are listening to a folk singer. Folk songs are songs that were made up by the common people.

farmers, and sailors all over the world. Folk songs are the songs that people often sing when they come together for a good time. They're the songs that people sing, hum, and whistle as they work. In fact, many folk songs were made up just to make work seem easier. They help to make a long, hard day go faster.

Israel

At a celebration in Israel, people do a lively, popular folk dance called the hora.

The square dance is one of the oldest of American folk dances.

United States

Dance away all

"Swing your partner, round you go!
Don't step on her pretty little toe!"
Back and forth, in and out, round and round go the
dancers as the caller tells them what to do. It's
Saturday night, and nearly everyone in town is
enjoying an old-fashioned American square dance.

Across the sea in Israel, a group of people are
enjoying a dance, too. The dancers have formed a big
circle. Each dancer's hands are stretched out to
touch the shoulders of the person on each side.
Three steps right—kick! Three steps left—kick! The
circle begins to move faster and faster. The dancers
flash by in a blur of bodies. It's the hora!

In Yugoslavia, the men of a small village are
dancing the teshkoto, or shepherd's dance. A big drum
beats slowly as the men move in a circle taking small
steps. Now the drum beats faster. The men leap high,
twirling their feet. *"Zivalee! Zivalee!"* ("Bravo!")
shout the women and children.

When people get together for a good time at a party,
a wedding, or on a holiday, they often dance. Many of
the dances they do are folk dances—dances that were
made up hundreds of years ago. These are dances that
never change.

Every country has its own folk dances. Usually they
are fast-moving dances that show that people are
happy—like the square dance, the hora, the teshkoto,
the Polish polka, and the Italian tarentella.

Riddle me this

The more you feed it,
the more it will grow high.
But if you give it water,
then it will quickly die.

What could it be? Some kind of animal that lives without water? A desert plant?

The answer is—fire.

That's a riddle, of course. An old, old riddle. Riddles are probably the oldest of all games. In ancient times, men who could make up and solve riddles were thought to be the best leaders and wisest men. Riddles were used to teach children many important facts of life. Almost everybody in the world plays the riddle game.

The Aborigines of Australia ask this riddle:
The strongest man cannot stand against me.
I can knock him down, yet I do not hurt him.
And he feels better because I have knocked him down!
What am I?
The answer is—sleep.

Here's an old English riddle that's also a rhyme:
Flour of England, fruit of Spain,
Met together in a shower of rain:
Put in a bag tied round with a string,
If you'll tell me this riddle, I'll give you a ring.
The answer is—a plum pudding.

People of India know this riddle:
I wear many coats,
And I have a hot temper!
What am I?
The answer is—an onion.

In Africa there's a riddle that goes:
Who is the old lady
that cries when she's knocked by a child?
The answer is—a drum.

And this is a riddle from Spain:
There's a lazy old woman with one tooth in her head.
But with that tooth, she gathers a crowd.
The answer is—a churchbell.

And one of the oldest riddles of all is this one:
What flies forever
And rests never?
The answer, of course, is—the wind.

Everywhere in the world, children love
to ask riddles and try to answer them.

United States

Wise words

In every country in the world there are old sayings that give good advice. These sayings are called proverbs.

Most proverbs are so old that no one knows when they were first said. Some proverbs suggest the best way to do something. Others tell how to get along with people. And some tell people how they should behave.

Proverbs are often much the same from one land to another. Many give the same advice in slightly different ways.

Rome: *Hunger is the best cook.*
India: *Hunger has no taste.*
France: *To a hungry man, there is no bad bread.*

These proverbs mean that if you are hungry enough, you'll eat anything. You won't care what it tastes like.

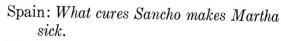

Spain: *What cures Sancho makes Martha sick.*
England: *One man's meat is another man's poison.*
France: *What is bad for one is good for another.*

These proverbs mean that people like different things. You may like something very much, but others may not like it.

England: *Haste makes waste.*
China: *Mistakes happen because of haste,
 never by doing a thing slowly.*
Spain: *Who pours water into a bottle
 with haste, spills more than he gets in.*

These proverbs mean that if you try to do something too quickly, you will not do it well.

Iran: *A sparrow in the hand is better
 than a hawk in the air.*
Rome: *A bird in the hand is worth two
 in the bush.*
Yugoslavia: *Oat bread today is better than
 cake tomorrow.*

These proverbs mean that it is best to be happy with what you have. Do not wish for something you may not get.

Poland: *He who digs a hole under others,
 falls into it himself.*
Bible: *Whoso diggeth a pit shall fall
 therein.*
Rome: *Treachery, in the end, betrays
 itself.*

These proverbs mean that if you do something bad to someone, something bad will happen to you.

United States

The round designs on this barn in Pennsylvania are hex signs to guard against bad luck and witch spells.

These fishermen wear masks to protect them from evil spirits and help them catch lots of fish.

Philippines

Good luck, bad luck

Some of us have only a tiny bit of it. Some of us have a lot of it. But almost all of us have some of it. What is it? It's superstition. At least that is what some of us call it.

Long ago, people didn't know much about the world—especially about natural events. They didn't know what causes thunder or an eclipse of the sun or the moon. They thought these events were brought about by evil forces. They also believed that certain actions or objects could bring good luck or bad luck. Because they didn't understand, they tried to make things work for them by means of magic. They had all sorts of charms, chants, and spells to make good things happen or to keep bad things from happening.

Today, few of us believe that thunder and eclipses are caused by evil forces. We can find no reason to believe that something is lucky or unlucky. We call such beliefs "superstitions."

But some of us carry a rabbit's foot for good luck. Others think it is bad luck to break a mirror or walk under a ladder. Some of us will not open an umbrella in the house or step on a crack in the sidewalk.

We say we don't *really* believe—that these are just superstitions. But we don't want to invite trouble. So we "knock on wood"—just in case.

Switzerland

This head, carved on a tree trunk, is supposed to bring good crops and keep bad luck away.

These pictures of wild horses, in Lascaux Cave
in France, were painted about 15,000 years ago.

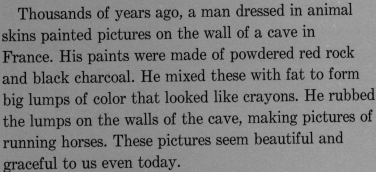

The Way We See It

Thousands of years ago, a man dressed in animal skins painted pictures on the wall of a cave in France. His paints were made of powdered red rock and black charcoal. He mixed these with fat to form big lumps of color that looked like crayons. He rubbed the lumps on the walls of the cave, making pictures of running horses. These pictures seem beautiful and graceful to us even today.

We need beauty around us. That's why we paint pictures and make statues. That's why we wear beads, bracelets, and earrings. That's why there is color and design in our clothes, our houses, our furniture, and most other things we own and use.

We all love beauty. But what seems beautiful to one person may not seem beautiful to another. We get our ideas of beauty from the culture we live in. What is beautiful depends upon the way we see it.

A South African woman decorates the wall around her house with secret tribal markings.

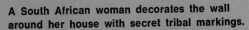

South Africa

A woman of the Ndebele tribe decorates the wall that surrounds her yard.

Eye-catching walls

There is a beautiful village about 30 miles from the city of Pretoria, South Africa. It stands in the middle of wild country called the bush. In the village, the people of the Ndebele tribe live in small huts made of clay and cow droppings. Each hut stands in a courtyard surrounded by a wall. What makes the village beautiful? It's the big, bright designs on the houses and courtyard walls.

All Ndebele women are artists. As soon as a wall is built, they decorate it. The women paint outlines in black, gray, or white. Then they fill in the design with blue, green, yellow, red, and other colors.

Each design and each color has a secret meaning. Only a few of the old people know the meanings. But everybody likes to look at the eye-catching walls.

In cities in the United States, other artists paint exciting pictures on other bare, ugly walls. These pictures show how the people of the neighborhood feel about themselves, about other people, and about the world around them.

United States

Neighborhood artists turn a drab wall into a painting everyone can enjoy.

Pictures to walk on

Every day, thousands of busy people hurry back and forth over city sidewalks. They hardly ever look down at the gray concrete beneath their feet—except to avoid tripping over a crack or a bump.

But in some cities, sidewalks are really something to see! Colored stones, pebbles, and tiles form patterns and pictures to walk on. Decorated sidewalks help to make Rio de Janeiro, Brazil, one of the most beautiful cities in the world.

Lisbon, Portugal, also has picture sidewalks. These pictures, made of tiny, colored tiles, show great events in Portuguese history.

Sidewalks don't have to be plain, gray concrete. They can be beautiful patterns, designs, and pictures to walk on. But first, people have to want them to be beautiful.

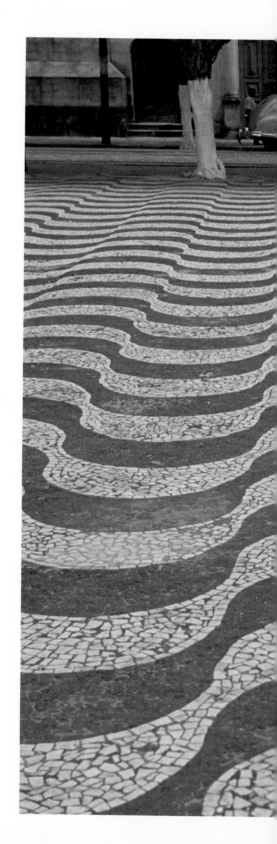

Brazil

Decorated sidewalks help make Rio de Janeiro a beautiful city.

Moving colors

For hundreds of years, fishermen have decorated their boats. Some fishermen like broad, colorful stripes or beautiful flowers on their boats. Others like pictures of saints or mermaids. Still others paint huge eyes on each side so the boat can "see" its way safely. Colors and pictures help to make plain workboats more personal and more attractive.

People everywhere like to decorate their cars, carts, bicycles, and animals. Even when we are on the move, we like to have color around us.

India

In the city of Chandigarh, drivers decorate pedicabs to attract customers.

Some people paint flowers on their cars because it pleases them.

United States

Portugal

Portuguese fishermen like to decorate
their boats with colorful stripes and designs.

Italy

On the island of Sicily, carts are
works of art for everyone to enjoy.

Underground palaces

Imagine you are riding down a flight of moving stairs. Suddenly you are deep underground. Instead of a dark, damp place, you are in a beautiful room. It is magnificent. It might be the inside of a palace. Where are you? You are in a subway station in Moscow, Russia.

Polished marble floors reflect the beautiful lights that hang from a decorated ceiling. Paintings cover the walls. Statues, stained-glass windows, and splashing fountains are everywhere.

Subway stations don't have to be dark and damp. Some of the stations in Moscow are so grand, people often visit them just to look around.

Russia

Beautiful lights and decorated ceiling and walls make this subway station in Moscow look like a palace.

Can you "read" the pictures?

Look at the elephant! Do you see the soldier on the prancing horse? No, it's not a parade. These are pictures painted on a house in India.

Other pictures tell about the family in the house—if you can "read" the pictures. For instance, a lotus flower means a wedding. And a picture of the god Siva and his wife Parvati means that a baby boy was born to the family.

People in many parts of the world decorate houses and other buildings. Some pictures show events in history. Some have a religious meaning. And some are designs that are supposed to have a magic power. But whatever the meaning, the pictures are nice to look at.

India

Pictures from Indian religious stories decorate the walls of this house.

Mexico

Pictures of events in Mexican
history decorate the library
at the University of Mexico.

South Africa

All Ndebele houses have
designs painted on them.

Which do you like best?

Some people like decorated things. They fill their houses with carved and painted furniture. They hang fancy lights from decorated ceilings. They put lots of pictures on the walls. They cover the floors with patterned rugs.

Other people like plain-looking things. They like rooms to look airy and roomy. They want their furniture to be quite plain and simple. They like polished wooden floors. They like bare walls and big windows.

Which do you like best?

Denmark

Some people think plain furniture, big windows, and lots of space make a room beautiful.

United States

Some people think painted furniture and soft carpets make a room beautiful.

Beauty is how we think of it

Every culture has its own kind of art. A temple carving in Taiwan is different from a carving on a temple in India. A Japanese painting is different from a French painting. And a Danish statue doesn't look at all like an African statue. All of these have beauty, but not for everybody.

Usually, we like one work of art better than another because it looks like what we think is beautiful. But we can enjoy works of art from any culture. What we need to know is that people have different ideas of what is beautiful.

Denmark

An artist shapes and carves a clay statue of a mother and her child.

Japan

Children watch an artist paint designs on a piece of silk stretched over a wooden frame.

Taiwan

Using a chisel and a mallet, an artist makes a woodcarving for a temple.

Beads and bracelets

In the steamy forests of Brazil, the Indians wear
hardly any clothes—or no clothes at all. But they
love to dress up. How do they do it? They wear
lots of jewelry.

But their jewelry isn't the kind that's made of gold,
silver, and jewels. These Indians use stones, bones,
teeth, claws, and feathers. They use the brightly
colored feathers of the toucan bird as ear ornaments.
And they make necklaces from the claws of jaguars and
other animals.

The Navaho Indians of the Southwestern United
States are famous for their jewelry. Skilled craftsmen
use silver and a blue-green jewel called a turquoise to
make beautiful necklaces, bracelets, and rings.

Everywhere in the world, people wear some kind
of jewelry to make themselves look more beautiful.

Brazil

In some parts of Brazil, the Indians hang bird feathers from their ears and wear necklaces made from the claws of animals.

United States

Navaho Indians like to make and wear silver and turquoise jewelry.

United States

Which one to wear? Women try to choose jewelry that matches the kind of clothes they are wearing.

Decorated skin—ouch!

It hurts to cut the skin or stick a pin in it. But some people don't care how much it hurts, if they think it makes them look beautiful!

In Mozambique, on the eastern coast of Africa, there are people who think that no woman is beautiful unless she has scars on her skin. So women here get artists to make cuts on their faces and backs. Then earth and herbs are rubbed into the cuts. The cuts heal slowly and leave a pattern of raised scars. This can hurt, but the women do it because they want to be beautiful.

The Berbers of North Africa think that decorated faces are prettier than plain faces. So a Berber woman makes a design on her face. To do this, she pokes tiny holes in her skin. Then she fills the holes with coloring matter.

In other places, men and children decorate their skins. We all have our own ideas about what is beautiful.

Morocco

Berber women decorate their faces with colored designs.

Mozambique

This woman has had her skin decorated with raised scars. Without these scars, she would not be considered beautiful.

How do you wear your hair?

We usually wear our hair in ways we think make us look our best. We also like to be in style. But hair styles change. What looks fine to us at one time, may look funny to us at another time.

A few years ago, most men and boys in the United States wore short hair. Those who wore long hair or beards looked strange. Today, long hair, beards, and mustaches are in style.

People in all parts of the world have their own ideas about hair styles. If hair styles look strange, it is probably because we aren't used to them.

This young Zulu girl wears her hair in a special way to show that she is not married.

South Africa

United States

Boys and girls wear their hair in several
ways. Long hair is now the most popular.

India

The Todas are a people who live in
southern India. The Toda women
wear their hair in long curls and
have fancy tattoos on their bodies.

Archaeology students work to uncover the skeleton
of an ancient Indian near Kampsville, Illinois.

People Watchers

Would you like to dig up the skeleton of someone who lived thousands of years ago? Or explore the bottom of the ocean for treasure from sunken ships? Or do things to help people live better and be happier? Those are things that "people watchers" do!

People watchers are men and women who are interested in people everywhere. Some people watchers are trying to find out about the very first people, millions of years ago. Some people watchers are interested in how people lived thousands or hundreds of years ago. Others study the ways that people now live, and work, and think. And still others work with individuals and families to help them solve their problems.

All this work is important and useful. The things that people watchers learn about us add to our knowledge of ourselves, and may help us find ways of making life better for people everywhere.

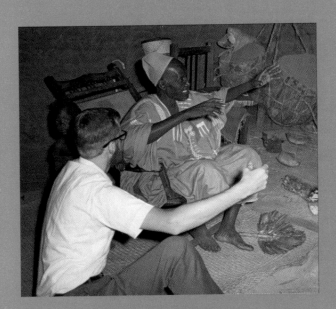

An anthropologist lives among the people he studies.

Learning about people everywhere

The way that a group of people live is called its culture. Each group of people has some ways of life that make it different from all other groups of people. Scientists called cultural anthropologists study the cultures of people everywhere.

A cultural anthropologist wants to know how people in a particular culture get their food, how they work and play, and how they worship. Why do they dress the way they do? What do they wonder about? What are they afraid of? What do they think is bad and good, or beautiful and ugly? How do they pass their culture on to their children?

To find out about such things, some cultural anthropologists travel to distant lands. They live with the people they study. They learn their customs, they eat their foods, they even help them with their work.

Other cultural anthropologists work closer to home, in their own countries. They study the ways of people who live in big cities and small towns.

Dr. Margaret Mead

Dr. Mead is a famous cultural anthropologist. She is the author of a book for children called *Anthropologists and What They Do.*

anthropologist studying African tribal life

Cultural anthropologists often
go to distant places and live
with the people they study.

museum diorama

Artists and sculptors work
with anthropologists to prepare
museum exhibits so that we can
see how other people live.

Learning about physical differences

Where did people come from? Why do people have different skin colors? Why are some groups of people taller or shorter than others? These are some of the questions that scientists called physical anthropologists want to answer.

Some physical anthropologists hunt for, and study, the bones of manlike creatures that lived millions of years ago. They try to find out how people have changed, how they have become the way they are.

Other physical anthropologists study living people. They look for answers to many questions. Why do people have curly hair, or straight hair, or kinky hair? Why do our heads have different shapes?

Dr. Louis Leakey

Dr. Leakey was a famous physical anthropologist. He discovered the bones of manlike creatures that scientists believe lived nearly two million years ago.

anthropologists searching for fossils

Some physical anthropologists search for fossils—the bones
◀ of prehistoric people. This is the Olduvai Gorge in Africa, where many fossils and ancient tools have been found.

archaeologists at work

Archaeologists and students are digging up an ancient Indian village in Illinois.

Learning about people of long ago

Scientists who study the things made by people who lived long ago are called archaeologists.

By digging in places where people once lived, archaeologists find houses, tools, dishes, weapons, and other objects. Sometimes they find marvelous works of art, such as statues and paintings. And sometimes they find cities that have been covered up for thousands of years. This digging is hard work, but it's like an exciting treasure hunt!

Archaeologists have discovered much of what we know about old civilizations. Now we can read about the daily life of the ancient Egyptians, the Aztecs, and other people.

(continued on page 276)

marking the age of the dig

Archaeologists mark the levels of the dig with pieces of string. Each lower level represents an earlier period in the life of the village.

student digger

Digging is hard, messy work. But it's fun. You never know what treasures you might find!

artifacts

Artifacts are things archaeologists look for when they dig—weapons, tools, plates, and pots used by the people of long ago. These artifacts are Indian arrowheads.

Learning about people of long ago
(continued from page 275)

For thousands of years, ships from many lands have sailed the waters of the world. Some of these ships—ancient Egyptian riverboats, Viking dragonships, Roman galleys, and Spanish treasure galleons—were sunk in terrible storms or in battles. Many of these ships carried cargoes of everyday objects. Others were full of treasures.

Underwater archaeologists hunt for such sunken ships. When they find one, they dive down, wearing special equipment. They take pictures and make charts. They search the wreck and the area around it.

Many beautiful works of art, weapons, coins, and other things have been found by underwater archaeologists. In some cases, they have even brought up entire ships!

treasures from the sea

A beautiful statue of a Greek god and a pile of gold coins are some of the exciting things that have been found beneath the sea.

bringing up a find

An underwater archaeologist brings up an ancient jar he has found on the ocean floor off the Shetland Islands.

underwater archaeologists at work

Archaeologists use long metal rods to divide a wreck into squares. They take pictures of the part of the ship in each square. The pictures are put together (above) to make a chart of the whole ship.

social worker and immigrants

Immigrants—people who have moved from one
country to another—face many new problems.
Social workers help these people adjust to
their new life. Here, a social worker meets
with a group of people who have come to
the United States from Puerto Rico. He is
showing them how to use American newspapers
to look for jobs and to find stores.

Learning about people's problems

Scientists called sociologists study how people live and work together. They try to find out why there is sometimes trouble between two groups of people living near each other. They study what happens to people who move to new places and change their ways of life.

Social workers are people who are trained to help individuals and families work out their problems. They help people to get food, clothing, and jobs. They help newcomers from other countries learn the ways and language of their new land. And they work with people in hospitals, schools, and prisons.

Psychologists are scientists who try to find out why people think and act as they do. Why do we sometimes get angry or sad with no real reason? Why are we afraid of some people or things?

All of these "people watchers" work in different ways to help us understand ourselves and others, and to help us have better lives.

social worker, teaching

A big part of a social worker's job may be the teaching of new skills. This social worker (on the right) is teaching English to a newcomer from Puerto Rico.

The French explorer Jacques Cartier meeting with
the Indians near what is now Quebec, Canada.

Living in Two Worlds

Imagine how surprised the Indians were when they first saw men from Europe. In the Indians' world, clothes were made of animal skins. Their tools and weapons were made of wood and stone. But these people with pale skins wore strange clothes made of something called cloth. And they had strange objects made of something called metal. To the Indians, they were men from another world!

In time, Indians and Europeans began to use things from each other's world. From the Indian world, Europe got pipes, tobacco, corn, and potatoes. From the European world, the Indians got cloth, metal tools, and new ideas. Both Indians and Europeans began to live in two worlds.

Today, most of us live in two worlds. One is the world of old familiar things we've always known. The other is the world of new ideas and inventions, new kinds of food and clothing, things that often come from other people and other lands. Everywhere, you can see the old and the new, side by side.

The old world and the new in India.

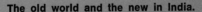

India

Men riding on elephants have been a common sight in India for thousands of years. Today, cars, trucks, and buses are common sights. Two worlds—the old and the new—are side by side.

Kenya

These two men are going to a big tribal celebration, like those held long ago. Their fancy feather headdresses are part of a traditional costume. But to get to the celebration on time, they depend on something from the world of today—bicycles.

United States

Ways to have fun are often borrowed from
other cultures. These Eskimo children
in Alaska are learning a dance borrowed
from Mexico—the Mexican hat dance.

United States

The hibachi (Japanese for "fire pot") is a small charcoal stove. It was used in Japan to heat houses. People in many parts of the world now use it for cooking.

Dressed in costumes like those their ancestors wore, these Polish-American children do a traditional folk dance at a festival in New Jersey.

United States

Ivory Coast

Many of these people are dressed in traditional clothing. Some still follow ancient tribal customs. But they worship in a modern church.

Botswana

This African mother wears a dress copied from those that German women wore more than 100 years ago. Her daughter's clothes are just like those worn today in Europe and the United States.

Mexico

Sometimes, people of today's world borrow ideas from the world of long ago. This modern house is decorated with ancient Aztec Indian designs.

When people from the same country move to another land, they often like to live together. This way they can keep their language and some old customs. These children in the Chinese section of Boston are doing an old Chinese dance.

United States

A modern, factory-made hydrofoil boat
zips across Lake Titicaca in Peru. It's
right out of today's world. But the Indians
who fish on the lake use reed boats that
are made by hand and belong to the
world of long ago.

Peru

Finland

Many of the people called Lapps still wear the bright clothing that is their traditional costume. Some still follow their reindeer herds, as their fathers did before them. But their fathers used sleds pulled by teams of reindeer. The sons travel in snowmobiles.

Ivory Coast

In the old African city of Abidjan, a shop advertises modern hair styles.

India

These farmers are harvesting wheat in an old-fashioned way —while listening to a modern, portable radio.

Japan

Hamburger stands have long been common in the United States. Now they're appearing in other countries, too.

New Words

Some of the words you have met in this book may be new to you. Many of them are words you'll meet again, so they are good words to know. Some are the names of countries that may be hard for you to say. Here are some of these words. Next to each word you are shown how to say it: **Aborigine** (ab uh RIJ uh nee). The part shown in capital letters is said a little more loudly than the rest of the word. Under each word, the meaning is given in a complete sentence.

Aborigine (ab uh RIJ uh nee)
The Aborigines are people whose ancestors were the first to live in Australia, long ago.

adobe (uh DOH bee)
Adobe is sun-dried brick. It is used as a building material.

Afghanistan (af GAN uh stan)
Afghanistan is a mountainous kingdom in southern Asia.

American Samoa (uh MEHR uh kuhn su MOH uh)
American Samoa is a group of islands in the South Pacific Ocean.

amphibian (am FIHB ee un)
An amphibian is an animal that lives both on land and in water.

ancient (AYN shuhnt)
Anything that belongs to times long past is ancient.

anthropologist (an thruh PAHL uh jihst)
An anthropologist is a scientist who studies people and the ways they live. A cultural anthropologist studies people's customs and beliefs. A physical anthropologist studies the development of human beings, the bones of prehistoric men, and the way living people look.

anthropology (an thruh PAHL uh jee)
Anthropology is the scientific study of people and their ways of life.

Apache (uh PACH ee)
The Apache are a tribe of Indians who live in the American Southwest.

Appalachia (ap uh LAY chuh)
Appalachia is the name given to a large area in the Appalachian Mountains in the Eastern United States.

archaeologist (ahr kee AHL uh jihst)
An archaeologist is a scientist who studies people who lived long ago and their ways of life.

archaeology (ahr kee AHL uh jee)
Archaeology is the scientific study of the tools, objects, customs, and beliefs of ancient people.

artifact (AHR tuh fakt)
An artifact is a thing that was made by a human being.

astronomer (uh STRAHN uh muhr)
An astronomer is a scientist who studies the stars and planets.

Bali (BAH lee)
Bali, an island in Southeast Asia, is part of the country of Indonesia.

bazaar (buh ZAHR)
In Asia, a bazaar is a section of a town where food, clothing, and other things are sold.

Botswana (boh TSWAH nah)
Botswana is a country in Africa.

Buddha (BOOD uh)
Buddha was the man who began the Buddhist religion.

Buddhist (BOOD ihst)
A Buddhist is a person who believes in the teachings of Buddha.

ceremony (SEHR uh moh nee)
A ceremony is the way people do things on special occasions such as weddings or funerals.

Ceylon (see LAHN)
Ceylon is an island country in the Indian Ocean. Its official name is Sri Lanka.

chemical (KEHM uh kuhl)
Chemicals are the stuff out of which all things are made. Gases and metals are chemicals.

civilization (sihv uh luh ZAY shun)
Civilization is the way of life of people who use art, science, and manners to help them live together peacefully and comfortably.

Coyote (ky OH tee or KY oht)
Coyote is a North American Indian hero about whom many tales are told. Sometimes he is a man and sometimes he is a coyote. (A coyote is a small wolf that lives in western North America.)

culture (KUHL chur)
A culture is the way of life, the art, and the beliefs of a group of people.

custom (KUHS tum)
A custom is the way a group has done something for a long time.

diorama (dy uh RAM uh)
A diorama is a small scene made by an artist or sculptor. It usually shows figures of people or animals in real-looking surroundings.

Ethiopia (ee thee OH pee uh)
Ethiopia is a mountainous country in northeastern Africa.

fossil (FAHS uhl)
A fossil is the hardened remains or traces of an ancient plant or animal.

Ganges (GAN jeez)
The Ganges is a river in India. People of the Hindu religion regard it as holy.

Ghana (GAH nuh)
Ghana is a country in western Africa.

hydrofoil (HY droh foyl)
A hydrofoil is a boat with fins on the bottom of the hull. At high speed, the fins lift the hull out of the water. This makes the boat go even faster.

icon (EYE kahn)
An icon is a picture of Christ, an angel, or a holy person, usually painted on wood or ivory.

immigrant (IM uh grunt)
An immigrant is a person who comes into another country to live.

incense (IHN sehns)
Incense is a mixture of woods and spices that gives off a sweet smell when it is burned.

Iraq (ee RAHK)
Iraq is an Arab country in Southwest Asia.

Islam (IHS luhm or ihs LAHM)
Islam is the religion that was begun by Mohammed

Korean (kaw REE uhn)
A Korean is a native of Korea, a country in eastern Asia.

Kuwait (koo WYT)
Kuwait is a small Arab country in Southwest Asia.

maize (mayz)
Maize is common corn. It is sometimes called Indian corn. Sweet corn and popcorn are kinds of maize. In England, maize is the name given to all kinds of corn.

mammal (MAM uhl)
A mammal is an animal that has live babies instead of laying eggs. A mother mammal feeds her baby with milk from her body.

Messiah (muh SY uh)
The Messiah, as foretold by the Jewish prophets in the Old Testament, will lead all the Jewish people to peace and freedom.

minaret (mihn uh REHT)
A minaret is a slender, high tower on a Moslem mosque.

minstrel (MIHN struhl)
A minstrel was a musician and singer who traveled from town to town hundreds of years ago.

Morocco (muh RAHK oh)
Morocco is a small, mountainous country in northern Africa.

Mohammed (moh HAM uhd)
Mohammed is the man who began the religion of Islam.

Moslem (MAHZ luhm or MAHS luhm)
A Moslem is a person who follows the religion of Islam, begun by Mohammed.

Mozambique (moh zuhm BEEK)
Mozambique is a small country on the southeastern coast of Africa. It is ruled by the European country of Portugal.

Navaho or **Navajo** (NAV uh hoh)
The Navaho are a tribe of Indians who live in the American Southwest. They are related to the Apache.

Nigeria (ny JEER ee uh)
Nigeria is a country in western Africa. It has more people than any other African country.

nirvana (nihr VAH nuh)
Nirvana is the state of perfect peace and happiness into which Buddhists hope to pass when they die.

nomad (NOH mad)
A nomad is a person who wanders from place to place and has no settled home.

Norse (nawrs)
The Norse were the people of ancient Norway, Sweden, and Denmark.

orthodox (AWR thuh dahks)
An orthodox member of a religious group accepts the old beliefs and ideas without wishing to change them.

Pakistan (PAK uh stan)
Pakistan is a country in southern Asia. It was once ruled as part of India.

Papua New Guinea (PAP oo uh noo GIN ee)
Papua New Guinea is part of the large island of New Guinea in the South Pacific Ocean. It is governed by Australia.

parliament (PAHR luh muhnt)
A parliament is a group of people who have been elected to make the laws for their country.

physical (FIHZ uh kuhl)
Physical means "of the human body."

Polynesian (pahl uh NEE zhuhn)
Polynesians are brown-skinned people
who live on many of the islands in the
Pacific Ocean.

prehistoric (pree hihs TAWR ihk)
Anything that took place before
written history is called prehistoric.

premier (prih MIHR or PREE mee uhr)
Premier is a title given to leaders
in some countries. It means "first."

proverb (PRAHV uhrb)
A proverb is a short, wise saying used
for a long time by many people.

psychologist (sy KAHL uh jihst)
A psychologist is a scientist who tries
to find the reasons why people behave
as they do.

pueblo (PWEHB loh)
A pueblo is an American Indian village
in the Southwest. The people who built
these adobe and stone villages are
called Pueblo Indians.

Pygmy (PIHG mee)
A Pygmy is one of a group of small,
dark-skinned people who live in parts
of central Africa. Pygmies are usually
between 4 and 5 feet tall.

social worker (SOH shuhl WUR kuhr)
A social worker tries to help people
better their living conditions.

sociologist (soh see AHL uh jihst)
A sociologist is a scientist who
studies how people live and work and
get along together. Sociologists want
to know the causes of individual and
group problems.

spiritual (SPEER uh chu uhl)
A spiritual is a type of religious song
made famous by Negroes in the
Southern United States.

Sumatra (soo MAH truh)
Sumatra is an island in southeastern
Asia. It is part of Indonesia.

synagogue (SIHN uh gawg)
Jews meet and worship in a building
called a synagogue.

Tahiti (tuh HEE tee)
Tahiti is an island in the South
Pacific Ocean.

Taiwan (ty WAHN)
Taiwan is an island off the coast of
China. Most of the people are Chinese.

Thailand (TY land)
Thailand is a country in Southeast
Asia. It was once called Siam.

torii (TAWR ee ee)
A torii is the gateway to a Japanese
Shinto shrine.

tortilla (tawr TEE yuh)
A tortilla is a thin, flat, round corn
cake eaten in Mexico, Central America,
and South America.

traditional (truh DISH uh nuhl)
A traditional thing is something that
has been handed down for many years.
It may be a belief, a kind of music,
clothing, or a way of doing something.

turquoise (TUR koyz or TUR kwoyz)
Turquoise is a blue or greenish-blue
stone often used to make jewelry.

Zaire (ZAH ihr)
Zaire is a country in the central part
of Africa.

Illustration Acknowledgments

The publishers of *Childcraft* gratefully acknowledge the courtesy of the following artists, photographers, publishers, agencies, and corporations for illustrations in this volume. When all the illustrations for a sequence of pages are from a single source, the inclusive page numbers are given. In all other instances, the page numbers refer to facing pages, which are considered as a single unit or spread. The words "(*left*)," "(*center*)," "(*top*)," "(*bottom*)," and "(*right*)" indicate position on the spread. All illustrations are the exclusive property of the publishers of *Childcraft* unless names are marked with an asterisk (*).

Cover: Standard binding: (*top right*) Field Educational Publications, Inc. (*); all other photos: E. S. Ross (*)
Cover: Aristocrat binding: (*top row left to right*) E. S. Ross (*); E. S. Ross (*); Field Educational Publications, Inc. (*); E. S. Ross (*); (*center row left to right*) E. S. Ross (*); Field Educational Publications, Inc. (*); E. S. Ross (*); E. S. Ross (*); Phiz Mezey (*); (*bottom row left to right*) E. S. Ross (*); E. S. Ross (*); E. S. Ross (*)

Pages Credits
2–3: Art: Bernard Arendt
8–9: see cover acknowledgment for Aristocrat binding
10–11: (*top center*) CHILDCRAFT photo by Donald Getsug; (*bottom left*) H. Fristedt from Carl Östman (*); (*right*) H. K. Bruske, Artstreet (*)
12–13: (*left*) Rolf Clipper from Carl Östman (*); (*right*) Fred Bruemmer (*)
14–15: (*left*) Leif-Erik Nygards, Artstreet (*); (*right*) H. K. Bruske, Artstreet (*)
16–17: (*top left*) Field Educational Publications, Inc. (*); (*top right*) Robert Davis, Artstreet (*); (*bottom left*) Costa Manos, Magnum (*); (*bottom right*) Gordon W. Gahan (*)
18–19: (*left*) E. S. Ross (*); (*right*) Ernest Baxter, Black Star (*)
20–21: (*left*) NASA (*); art: Gordon Laite
22–25: Art: David Palladini
26–27: Art: Max Ranft
28–29: Art: George M. Suyeoka
30–31: Art: Gordon Laite
32–35: Art: Herb Kawainue Kane
36–37: Art: George M. Suyeoka
38–41: Art: Leo and Diane Dillon
42–45: Art: Alex Ebel
46–47: (*left*) M. Daspet (*); (*right*) Al Abrams (*)
48–49: (*left*) Fred Bruemmer (*); art: Tak Murakami
50–51: (*left*) Al Abrams (*); art: Tak Murakami
52–53: (*left*) Victor Englebert, De Wys, Inc. (*); art: Tak Murakami
54–55: (*left*) Field Educational Publications, Inc. (*); art: Tak Murakami
56–57: (*left*) Ian Berry, Magnum (*); art: Tak Murakami
58–59: (*left*) Marc & Evelyne Bernheim, Woodfin Camp, Inc. (*); (*right*) Pictorial Parade (*)
60–61: (*top*) Dennis McGilvray (*); (*right*) Ted Speigel, Black Star (*)
62–63: (*left*) James Sugar (*); (*top center*) Sabine Weiss, Rapho Guillumette (*); (*center right*) Peter Arnold

(*); (*right*) John Launois, Black Star (*)
64–65: (*left*) Wayne Miller, Magnum (*); (*right*) Banyan Productions Singapore (*)
70–71: (*left*) Milt & Joan Mann (*); (*right*) Alan Band Associates (*)
72–73: (*left*) Jean-Pierre Laffont, Gamma (*); (*right*) Brian Seed, Black Star (*); (*bottom*) Harrison Forman (*)
74–75: (*right*) J. R. Eyerman, Black Star (*); art: Michael Hampshire
76–77: (*top*) Brian Seed, Black Star (*); (*bottom left*) E. S. Ross (*); (*bottom right*) Harry Redl, Black Star (*)
78–79: Art: Michael Hampshire
80–81: (*center*) Mark Barinholtz (*); (*top right*) Jordan Penkower, EPA (*); (*bottom right*) Gene Harris, Meyers Photo-Art (*); art: Michael Hampshire
82–83: (*top right*) Costa Manos, Magnum (*); (*bottom left*) Costa Manos, Magnum (*); art: Michael Hampshire
84–85: (*top right*) Robert Davis, Artstreet (*); (*bottom*) Robert Davis, Artstreet (*); art: Michael Hampshire
86–87: (*top right*) Alan Band Associates (*); (*bottom left*) H. Fristedt from Carl Östman (*); (*bottom right*) Harrison Forman (*); art: Michael Hampshire
88–89: (*left*) Anthony Howarth, Woodfin Camp, Inc. (*); (*top right*) Rolf Clipper from Carl Östman (*); (*bottom right*) Jean L. Briggs, Memorial University of Newfoundland (*)
90–91: Art: Jack Lefkowitz
92–93: (*left*) Huntington Library and Art Gallery, San Marino, California (*); (*right*) CHILDCRAFT photo
94–95: (*top*) Educational Development Center, Inc. (*); art: Denver Gillen
96–97: (*bottom*) David Moore, Black Star (*); art: Denver Gillen
98–99: (*left*) Leif-Erik Nygards, Artstreet (*); (*center*) Gene Harris, Meyers Photo-Art (*); (*right*) CHILDCRAFT Photo
100–101: (*top center*) J. Alex Langley, DPI (*); (*top right*) Vivian M. Peevers from Peter Arnold (*); (*bottom*) Wide World (*); art: Denver Gillen
102–103: (*left*) Sven-Eric Hedin from Carl Östman (*); (*right*) Dan Budnik, Woodfin Camp Inc. (*); art: Denver Gillen
104–105: (*right*) Loren McIntyre, Woodfin Camp, Inc. (*); (*bottom*) Burt Glinn, Magnum (*); art: Denver Gillen
106–107: (*center*) Robert Davis, Artstreet (*); (*bottom*) Toshio Watanabe, DPI (*); art: Denver Gillen
108–109: (*left*) David Muench (*); (*right*) Artstreet (*)
110–111: (*top center*) E. S. Ross (*); (*top right*) Field Educational Publications, Inc. (*); (*bottom left*) Harrison Forman (*); art: Joann Daley
112–113: (*left*) Loren McIntyre, Woodfin Camp, Inc. (*); art: Joann Daley
114–115: (*top left*) CHILDCRAFT photo by Donald Getsug; (*bottom left*) Bill Strode, Black Star (*); art: Joann Daley
116–117: (*left*) Artstreet (*); (*center*) Marc Riboud, Magnum (*); (*right*) Artstreet (*)
118–119: (*bottom*) CHILDCRAFT photo by Gilles Peress, Magnum; art: Joann Daley
120–121: (*left*) Winnebago Industries, Inc. (*); (*right*) Frederick Figall, Artstreet (*)
122–123: (*left*) Bernard Hermann, Gamma (*); (*top right*) Harrison Forman (*); (*bottom right*) Howard Sochurek from Peter Arnold (*)
124–125: (*top*) CHILDCRAFT photo by Sabine Weiss, Rapho Guillumette; art: Joann Daley
126–127: (*left*) Erich Lessing, Magnum (*); (*right*) BBM Associates (*)
128–129: (*right*) Bruce Davidson, Magnum (*); (*bottom*) Kay Honkanen from Carl Östman (*); art: Michael Hampshire
130–131: (*right*) Artstreet (*); (*center*) Loren McIntyre, Woodfin Camp, Inc. (*); art: Michael Hampshire
132–133: (*left*) BBM Associates (*); (*center*) Horst Munzig, Woodfin Camp, Inc. (*); (*right*) Foto A.G.E. from Carl Östman (*)
134–135: (*left*) E. S. Ross (*); art: Michael Hampshire
136–137: (*top*) CHILDCRAFT photo; (*bottom*) PHOTRI (*)
138–139: (*left*) Ted Speigel, Black Star (*); Bruno Barbey,

Magnum (*); (*right*) A. Gutierrez from Carl Östman (*); art: Michael Hampshire

140–141: (*left*) Dennis McGilvray (*); (*top right*) E. S. Ross (*); art: Michael Hampshire

142–143: (*left*) David Seymour, Magnum (*); (*right*) E. S. Ross (*)

144–145: (*left*) Milt & Joan Mann (*); (*right*) H. K. Bruske, Artstreet (*); (*bottom*) Burt Glinn, Magnum (*); art: Denver Gillen

146–147: (*left*) J. Alex Langley, DPI (*); art: Denver Gillen

148–149: (*left*) Alan Band Associates (*); (*top and bottom right*) Jerry Cooke (*)

150–151: (*left*) David Bier Studios from Miller Services (*); (*right*) Dan Budnik, Woodfin Camp, Inc. (*); art: Denver Gillen

152–153: (*right*) Jerry Cooke (*); art: Denver Gillen

154–155: (*left*) Adam Woolfitt, Woodfin Camp, Inc. (*); (*left center*) Fred Bruemmer (*); Jerry Cooke (*); (*bottom center*) Marc Riboud, Magnum (*); (*right*) Robert Glaze, Artstreet (*); art: Denver Gillen

158–159: (*top right*) Victor Englebert, De Wys, Inc. (*); (*bottom right*) E. S. Ross (*); art: Denver Gillen

160–161: Yannis Scouroyannis (*)

162–163: (*top*) Fred Fehl (*); (*left*) Stratford Festival Theater (*); (*bottom*) Victor Englebert, De Wys, Inc.

164–165: (*left*) The National Portrait Gallery, London (*); (*right*) Wulff Ligges, Van Cleve Photography (*)

166–167: (*top center*) Field Educational Publications, Inc. (*); (*bottom right*) E. S. Ross (*); art: Denver Gillen

168–169: (*top*) Victor Englebert, De Wys, Inc. (*); art: Denver Gillen

170–171: Jerry Cooke (*)

172–173: (*left*) Jacques Jangoux (*); (*top center*) Fred Ward, Black Star (*); (*bottom center*) Colin Davey, Transworld Feature Syndicate (*)

174–175: (*left*) Wulff Ligges, Van Cleve Photography (*); (*top right*) Hal Barkley, Miller Services (*); art: Denver Gillen

176–177: (*top left*) Werner Wolff, Black Star (*); (*bottom left*) H. Grafingholt, Van Cleve Photography (*); art: Denver Gillen

178–179: (*left*) Pictorial Parade (*); (*right*) Banyan Productions Singapore (*)

180–181: (*center*) Hiroshi Morimoto, BBM Associates (*); (*right*) Dennis McGilvray (*); art: Roland Des-Combes

182–183: (*center*) Milt & Joan Mann (*); (*right*) Ted Spiegel, Black Star (*); art: Roland DesCombes

184–185: (*center*) Gordon W. Gahan (*); (*right*) Mondadori Press from Pictorial Parade (*); art: Roland Des-Combes

186–187: (*center*) Banyan Productions Singapore (*); (*right*) Dennis McGilvray (*); art: Roland DesCombes

188–189: (*center*) Victor Englebert, De Wys, Inc. (*); (*right*) Dennis McGilvray (*); art: Roland DesCombes

190–191: (*right*) Jim Collins (*); art: Roland DesCombes

192–193: (*right*) Costa Manos, Magnum (*); art: Roland Des-Combes

194–195: (*center*) Milt & Joan Mann (*); (*right*) John Nicholais, Woodfin Camp, Inc. (*); art: Roland DesCombes

196–197: (*right*) E. S. Ross (*); art: Roland DesCombes

198–199: (*left*) The British Museum, London (*); (*right*) Annette Donner, Van Cleve Photography (*)

200–201: (*left*) Burt Glinn, Magnum (*); (*center*) E. S. Ross (*); (*right*) V. Lefteroff, De Wys, Inc. (*); (*bottom left*); art: Tak Murakami

202–203: (*bottom*) Annette Donner, Van Cleve Photography (*); art: Tak Murakami

204–205: (*left*) Toram Kahana from Peter Arnold (*); (*center*) Michael Manheim (*); art: Tak Murakami

206–207: (*top*) PHOTRI (*); (*right*) E. S. Ross (*); (*bottom*) Field Educational Publications, Inc. (*)

208–209: Richard Harrington (*)

210–211: (*top right*) PHOTRI (*); art: Tak Murakami

212–213: Morton Beebe (*)

214–215: (*numbered photos at right*) (1) WORLD BOOK photo; (2) Robert H. Glaze, Artstreet (*); (3 and 4) Milt & Joan Mann (*)

218–219: (*left*) St. Augustine Chamber of Commerce (*); (*right*) Field Educational Publications, Inc. (*)

220–221: E. S. Ross (*)

222–223: (*top*) E. S. Ross (*); (*center*) Field Educational Publications, Inc. (*); (*bottom left*) E. S. Ross (*); (*bottom center*) Field Educational Publications, Inc. (*)

224–225: (*right*) CHILDCRAFT photo by Sabine Weiss, Rapho Guillumette; art: Joann Daley

226–227: (*right*) E. S. Ross (*); art: Joann Daley

228–229: (*top left*) Loren McIntyre, Woodfin Camp, Inc. (*); (*bottom left*) Emil Schulthess, Black Star (*); (*bottom right*) Isabel Robins, Miller Services (*); art: Joann Daley

230–231: (*left*) CHILDCRAFT photo by Robert Crandall (*right*) David W. Hamilton, DeWys, Inc. (*)

232–233: Illustration by N. C. Wyeth from *The Boy's King Arthur* by Sydney Lanier; © 1917, renewed 1945, Charles Scribner's Sons (*), (illustration from the collection of Jack Webb (*), WORLD BOOK photo by E. Cornachio)

234–235: Illustration by Arthur Rackham from *Aesop's Fables*, Franklin Watts, Inc. (*)

236–237: David W. Hamilton, De Wys, Inc. (*)

238–239: (*top*) Gordon W. Gahan (*); art: Denver Gillen

240–241: CHILDCRAFT photo

242–243: Art: Jack Lefkowitz

244–245: (*top*) PHOTRI (*); (*bottom left*) Philip Boucas, Colorific (*); (*right*) Philip Boucas, Colorific (*)

246–247: (*left*) Jean Vertut (*); (*right*) E. S. Ross (*)

248–249: (*top*) E. S. Ross (*); (*bottom*) John Weber (*)

250–251: Emil Schulthess, Black Star (*)

252–253: (*top*) Field Educational Publications, Inc. (*); (*bottom left*) Rondal Partridge, BBM Associates (*); (*center*) Michael Reed (*); (*bottom right*) Robert Davis, Artstreet (*)

254–255: Novosti from Madeline Grimoldi (*)

256–257: (*left*) Dennis McGilvray (*); (*top right*) WORLD BOOK Photo; (*bottom right*) E. S. Ross (*)

258–259: (*left*) Thomas Nebbia, Woodfin Camp, Inc. (*); (*right*) Phiz Mezey (*)

260–261: (*left*) WORLD BOOK photo; (*top and bottom right*) Milt & Joan Mann (*)

262–263: (*top right*) Esther Henderson (*); (*bottom*) CHILDCRAFT photo; art: Michael Hampshire

264–265: (*left*) E. S. Ross (*); art: Michael Hampshire

266–267: (*left*) E. S. Ross (*); (*top right*) CHILDCRAFT photo; art: Michael Hampshire

268–269: (*left*) D. R. Baston, Illinois Foundation of Archaeology (*); (*right*) E. S. Ross (*)

270–271: (*left*) WORLD BOOK photo by Ken Heyman (*); (*top right*) E. S. Ross (*); (*bottom right*) CHILDCRAFT photo, courtesy Field Museum of Natural History, Chicago

272–273: Ian Berry, Magnum (*)

274–275: (*top and bottom left*) D. R. Baston, Illinois Foundation of Archaeology (*); (*top and bottom right*) Franklin McMahon, Jr., Illinois Foundation of Archaeology (*)

276–277: (*top left*) Raymond V. Schoder, S.J., Courtesy Archaeological Museum, Athens (*); (*bottom left*) Flip Schulke, Black Star (*); (*center*) Flip Schulke, Black Star (*); (*right*) Flip Schulke, Black Star (*); (*bottom*) John Veltri from Michael L. Katzev (*)

278–279: Esther Parada (*)

280–281: (*left*) Three Lions (*); (*right*), Mondadori Press from Pictorial Parade (*)

282–283: (*left*) M. Philip Kahl, Jr., Black Star (*); (*right*) Mondadori Press from Pictorial Parade (*)

284–285: (*left*) Fred Leavitt (*); (*right*) Fred Ward, Black Star (*); (*bottom*) CHILDCRAFT photo

286–287: (*top left*) Marc & Evelyne Bernheim, Woodfin Camp, Inc. (*); (*top right*) Eliot Elisofon, *Life* © Time Inc. (*); (*bottom left*) E. S. Ross (*); Owen Franken, Stock, Boston (*)

288–289: (*left*) Bill Ray, *Life* © Time Inc. (*); (*right*) G. Ronn from Carl Östman (*)

290–291: (*top left*) Mondadori Press from Pictorial Parade (*); (*bottom left*) Marc & Evelyne Bernheim, Woodfin Camp, Inc. (*); (*right*) Mack Law, Photofind (*)

Index

This index is an alphabetical list of the important topics covered in this book. It will help you to find information given in both words *and* pictures. Each topic is indexed in a number of ways. For example, if you want to know about Eskimos, look up the word Eskimo. Under this word you will find such topics as clothing, family, food, and so on. Or, if you want to know about clothing, look up the word clothing. Under this word you will find such topics as Arab, Eskimo, Japanese, and so on. To help you understand what an entry means, there is often a helping word in parentheses. For example, **Greek Orthodox** (religious group). If there are *also* pictures, you will see the words *with pictures* after the page number. For example, **superstition,** 245, *with pictures.* If there is *only* a picture, you will see the word *picture* before the page number. For example, **bicycle factory,** *picture,* 133.